ON THE ROAD

THE QUEST FOR STAMPS

STEPHEN R. DATZ

GENERAL PHILATELIC CORPORATION
LOVELAND, COLORADO

FIRST EDITION

The episodes portrayed in this book are based on actual incidents. In most cases, characters' names, identities, locations, and other relevant details have been fictionalized to protect individual privacy. Therefore, any resemblance to actual persons, living or dead, locales, or events is purely coincidental.

ISBN: 0-88219-025-3

Cover design: Mike Jenson
Cover painting: Stephen C. Datz

Manufactured in the United States of America

Published by General Philatelic Corporation
Post Office Box 402
Loveland, Colorado 80539

Philatelic Books by Stephen R. Datz

THE DATZ PHILATELIC INDEX

ON THE ROAD

TOP DOLLAR PAID!

THE WILD SIDE

U.S. ERRORS CATALOGUE

Acknowledgements

I am grateful to all who assisted in making this book a reality. Thanks to Steven Rod, Jacques Schiff Jr., and John Hotchner for their criticisms, suggestions, and advice. And thanks to James Magruder for his kind words and continued encouragement.

Thanks to Charles and Susan Deaton, Bob Dumaine, and Joe Savarese for sharing their recollections of incidents.

And a tip of the hat to Monte Brown, Walter Israel, Abbott Lutz, and Bill Pickles, all of whom it has been a privilege to know.

There comes the time in every manuscript's life when the real work begins, the seemingly endless rounds of final shaping, editing, and proofreading. Thanks, again, to Muriel Olson for her able assistance in this department and, also, for her encouragement.

Thanks to son Stephen for creating the painting used on the cover, and to Mike Jenson for the graphic design work.

And last, and most importantly, thanks to wife Susan for proofreading and general suggestions, and for her endless patience, not only during the preparation of this book, but during all those years when I was on the road.

Author's Notes

Between the years 1961 and 1985, I operated my business in Denver, Colorado, including the period between 1979 and 1985, when I was vice president of Scott Philatelic Corporation. Since 1985, I have operated my business from Loveland, Colorado, which is located about 55 miles north of Denver. Some chapters refer to my leaving from Denver on a trip, others from Loveland. Since the chapters are not arranged in chronological order, references to departure points are intermixed.

Technically, there are two kinds of stamp shows: a bourse, composed of dealers only, and an exhibition, which includes stamp exhibits as well as dealers. For the sake of convenience, I've used the term "bourse" to refer to the dealer section of both kinds of shows.

Any resemblance between the following names of characters or businesses (listed below in alphabetical order) that appear in this book and names of actual persons or businesses is purely coincidental: American National Coin Company, Johnny Angel, Paul Ballard, Burrito Grande, Charlie Byers, Cal Carrson, Cascade Mountain Stamp Company, Gary Casey, Edson Chapman, Stuart Cremona, Evelyn Cromwell, Maggie Daly, Matt Daly, Carleen Griggs, Rafael Griswold, Donovan Kurtz, Kurtz Capital Corporation, Last Chance Cafe, Billy Masterson, Norbert Dean McCall, Ruth Michaels, Amanda Moss, Mike Moss, Amy Proctor, Clark Sawyer, Tom Shelby, Cheri Slocum, Les Slocum, Eliot Warfield, White Peak Stamp Company, Alma Willoughby, James Willoughby, Nelson Wolfe, and Rollo Worthington.

Prologue

On a Sunday afternoon at a show not long ago, a casually dressed, middle-aged man stopped at my booth and spent a long time carefully browsing through my stock.

"Anything in particular you're looking for?" I asked.

"I never know what'll strike my fancy, so I just look at everything, thanks. Say, do you ever get any large lots or collections you'd sell at a good price?"

"Sure, but I don't take them to shows. They're too bulky."

"I'm trying to build a stock," he said. "Thought I'd get into the stamp business when I retire. Been planning to do it for years. Figured it'd be a lot of fun traveling around the country—maybe even overseas—buying and selling lots of stamps, meeting lots of people, seeing lots of exhibits, and all of it tax deductible." His fingers flicked through a box of stockcards as he spoke. Occasionally, he extracted a stamp for closer inspection.

"I can't wait to get started," he said.

The dream of being a stamp dealer brought a smile to my face. I'd lusted after the same dream myself—a long time ago. And I'd been down the road many miles since then. *It's going to be great!* I remember thinking of the travel-poster existence I imagined: jetting away to distant cities, handling rare stamps every day, dining out every night, leading a life of adventure. Every boy who has ever dreamed of running away to join the circus knows how bewitching the fantasy is, and how glorious the sense of anticipation.

That quiet Sunday afternoon, while the middle-aged man looked through my stock, the memories came flooding back—the high points and low points, the headaches and pleasures. . . .

Chapter 1

SWEPEX. Dallas, Texas. April 3, 1981.

The first clue I had that anything was wrong was the loud, anguished groan of metal as a large section of ductwork broke through the ceiling above the center of the grand ballroom. My booth stood against a far wall. I had been chatting with Monte Brown, whose booth was next to mine, when we heard the sound. We looked up to see what was wrong. The ductwork hung precariously suspended, its downward path slowed by the maze of wires and tubing normally concealed above the ceiling tiles. It groaned as it came through the tiles, a protesting, wrenching sound of metal twisting and being torn from metal. At the same time, roofing gravel, insulation, and ceiling tiles crashed down on luckless dealers below.

Charlie Deaton was doing business at a nearby table when he heard the violent noise and saw debris tumble onto his table. Water, too, poured down in a huge stream. Charlie's wife, Susan, dove for cover beneath one of their tables, while he scrambled to get back to his booth. A couple of nearby dealers reacted instantly, pulling Charlie's table out from under the path of falling water, saving most of his stamps. Though water had cascaded onto the tabletop, it hadn't had time to penetrate beneath the glass display cover and ruin any stamps.

A hush fell over the ballroom. Startled by the crashing noise and falling debris, the room held its breath for a long moment. Then it came alive with urgent voices. Instinctively, I looked up, thinking, *Is the whole roof going to come down? Why did it suddenly cave in for no apparent reason?* The ceiling above my head looked solid and in no danger of collapsing. Only the section in the center of the room had fallen.

An instant later, while the bourse still struggled to comprehend what had happened, the room went completely black, as devoid of light as the inside of a black cat on a moonless night. My first thought was to grab my stamps and get out. But I realized it would be impossible to pack all my stock and move it out in the darkness. The only thing I could do was secure my stamps in the locking cabinet behind me and leave the room immediately. Fortunately, it was near closing time, and no customers were at my table.

"You still there?" I asked Monte.

"Yeah," he replied. "What the hell's going on?"

"I don't know, but I just hope the whole roof doesn't cave in."

I lifted the plexiglass that covered my display and, feeling my way, quickly gathered stockcards of stamps into a pile that I held with my left hand. I used my right hand to search the tabletop until satisfied that I had everything. Then I turned, felt for the locker, plopped the stockcards onto a shelf, closed the door, and turned the key that dangled in the handle. That done, I asked, "Need any help, Monte?"

"No, I'm okay." I could hear him groping for his stamps but couldn't see him in the darkness.

About that time, someone slowly approached, flicking a cigarette lighter on and off every few seconds, just long enough to get his bearings as he made his way down the aisle. When he reached Monte and me, he left the lighter on.

"You guys okay?" he asked.

"So far," Monte said.

"You know what happened?" I asked.

"No," he said. "I'd be glad to stick around for a minute until you get your stuff put away."

"Thanks," Monte said, furiously gathering his stamps and covers in the flickering yellow light. Elsewhere in the ballroom, confused, frightened dealers struggled to secure their stocks. Voices called to one another, and, like fireflies, tiny cigarette lighter flames danced eerily in the dark, cavernous ballroom. No one knew what had happened, or what might yet happen. Each interpreted events in his own way.

Jacques Schiff Jr. later told me his first thought was that an airplane had crashed on or near the hotel, which was located near Love Field. I thought the hotel had experienced a structural failure and feared the whole building might collapse at any moment.

"You'd better hurry," I said, suddenly feeling claustrophobic. "Who knows what will happen next?"

"I'm going as fast as I can," Monte said. "I'll just be another minute. You might as well go. There's nothing you can do here."

"Are you sure?"

"Yes."

"I'd be careful with that lighter," I said to the good Samaritan. "What if there's a broken gas main?" I visualized the ballroom exploding in a giant ball of flame.

"I never thought of that," he replied. And that possibility underscored the wisdom of leaving the room quickly.

I headed beyond the pale glow of the cigarette lighter toward the front entrance. All I had to do was follow the wall my booth backed up against, turn left, then follow that wall to the exit. As I carefully moved forward, I heard the frenzied murmurs of people clearing their tables or trying to find their way out.

As I made my way, I literally bumped into Abbott Lutz. He clutched a wooden frame under one arm and held a cigarette lighter in his other hand. I recognized the frame. It contained the inverted Jenny that had been on display just inside the front door. It occurred to me that anyone could have snatched it from its easel and disappeared into the darkness.

"The entrance is the other way," I said to Abbott, who was headed toward the back of the room.

"I know," he said. "I had to get my invert. Now I've gotta get back to my table and finish up."

"Okay, see you later." We both disappeared into the blackness. Joe Savarese, Executive Director of the American Stamp Dealers Association under whose auspices SWEPEX was held, later told me that he saw Abbott calmly writing up an order for a customer by the glow of his cigarette lighter.

"Don't you know that lighter could explode if it gets too hot?" Joe said.

"Oh, it'll be all right," Abbott replied, seemingly unaffected by the chaos.

On my way to the front entrance, I ran into Walter Israel.

"Steve, is this exciting or what?" he exclaimed. Walter, in his mid-twenties at the time, traveled the show circuit selling advertising in Scott Catalogues for Scott Publishing Company.

"C'mon, Walter, let's get out of here." I made no attempt to hide the urgency in my voice. What Walter found thrilling, I found frightening.

We went out the main entrance. The foyer outside the ballroom was just as black as the ballroom.

"Follow me," Walter said. "I think I know the way to the lobby."

"You *think* you know?"

"Well, I'm pretty sure."

Oh, great, I thought, *the blind leading the blind.* Still, there was no use staying where we were.

"Okay, let's go," I said.

We inched our way down the hallway in the direction Walter thought the lobby should be. Shortly, we came upon a pool of light cast by a pair of emergency spots mounted high on the wall. A group of people huddled in the light, like fish in the eddy of a swift stream.

"Hi," Walter said, "Anyone know what happened?"

"Not for sure," a man volunteered, "Someone said something about a tornado."

I hadn't thought of a tornado, and the idea sent a fresh wave of fear through me. I knew how terrible tornados could be. I had seen them close-up on the eastern plains of Colorado. I knew that if a tornado hit the hotel full force, nothing would be left. I hoped the blackout wasn't a prelude to something worse.

An overwhelming sense of danger seized me. "C'mon, Walter, we've gotta get out of here—*now!*" I grabbed his arm above the elbow to emphasize my point. "You folks better find shelter, too."

"We're not sure which way the lobby is," one said.

"The ballroom is back the way we came," I said. "We're pretty sure the lobby is the other way, down the hall."

"Okay, we'll follow you."

We proceeded as rapidly as we could in the darkness, occasionally running into people coming from the opposite direction.

"Lobby back the way you came?" I asked one.

"Yup, just keep going," he replied.

"Thanks," I said, and we pushed on.

Finally, we saw the lobby up ahead, dim and full of people. When we reached it, our little band quickly dispersed. Walter and I headed for the front door.

Outside, the sky boiled. Its dark underbelly seethed with murderous pale greens and yellows that I recognized as tornado trademarks. Fierce wind lashed nearby trees and pelted our faces with rain. There was no way of knowing whether the tornado had passed or was still approaching. All I knew was that the hotel hadn't yet suffered a direct hit or it wouldn't be standing.

"What now?" Walter asked.

"Go to our rooms," I said. "Maybe there'll be some news on the radio or TV."

We headed around the exterior of the motel to find our rooms. It was one of those affairs, commonly known as motor hotels, that rise only a couple of stories off the ground, but have sprawling wings. My room was located on the second floor toward the end of one wing.

"Jeez, Walter, will you look at that!" I exclaimed, as we reached the room. The violent wind had peeled a section of veneer the length of the door, from top to bottom, as easily as you might pull the skin off a banana. The exposed ragged-edged, foot-wide strip of dark, wet wood looked like an open wound against the pastel color of the door.

"It takes one helluva wind to strip veneer like that," I said, inserting my key and turning the door handle. Behind us, trees danced and swayed in the wind, and thunder rumbled in the distance. The force of the wind swept the door open and gusted into the room, urging us along. I pushed the door shut and turned on the TV, forgetting the power was out.

"Now what?" Walter asked.

"Wait, I guess. There's not much else to do."

So we waited. When the power came on, we learned that Dallas had been hit by a destructive windstorm preceded by torrential rains, Fortunately, the motel hadn't been in the direct path of the tornado. In the windowless ballroom, we had been unaware that a storm raged outside, until the weight of accumulated water caused the roof to cave in.

Later, I learned that Joe Savarese, Jacques Schiff Jr. and other ASDA personnel worked tirelessly in the aftermath of the storm to clear the ballroom, arrange a secure storage room for dealers' stocks, and assist dealers in physically moving their stocks. To the credit of the trade and the public, no one panicked and no thefts were reported.

By the next day, the area directly beneath the cave-in had been roped off and the affected dealers moved to new locations. When Charlie Deaton returned to the spot where his table had been the day before and looked up, he could see daylight. The show went on. Dealers traded war stories about what they'd done when the bourse went black. And I went out and bought a flashlight.

Chapter 2

Shows and buying trips are the two reasons for being on the road in the stamp business.

Stamp shows make economic sense because they condense a great amount of traffic into both a small area and a short span of time. Shows allow out-of-town dealers to broaden their markets and freshen their stocks with purchases from other dealers. Cash and stamps change hands in a flurry of activity, which, like cross-pollination, keeps the stamp industry vigorous.

A sense of nervous anticipation precedes each show. Thoughts, like a flock of startled birds, take flight as opening time approaches. *Did I bring the right stamps? Are they priced too high or too low? Have I identified everything properly?* (Nothing is more embarrassing than having a collector correct you on a misidentified item, but it's happened to the best of us.) *Have I forgotten something?* (You always forget to take something.) *What if no one buys anything? Will I clear expenses? Will I make a profit?*

At the same time, adrenalin pumps. You're fired by a bright, warm sense of expectation and adventure, filled with enthusiasm and energy. There are deals to be done, profits to be made, old friends to be greeted, and new stock to found. There's a sense of urgency, a desire to rush from table to table to locate and buy all the gems before your competitors find them.

There is great camaraderie among dealers on the show circuit. You share information, gain knowledge, watch each other's backs, tell jokes, and do the town when the day's over and business has been good.

Just as stamp shows are ideal for reaching a broader market, buying trips are great for obtaining stamps from diverse sources.

Collectors often feel uncomfortable selling stamps back to the dealers they bought from. Perhaps they're embarrassed to admit they're parting with what they've bought from him, or that by leaving the hobby they're committing a breach of faith. Perhaps they want to avoid the discomfort of having to refuse a price that is less than expected from an old friend. And there is the school of thought, not necessarily true, that distant dealers pay more than local dealers. So, ironically, it is distance itself that often brings buyer and seller together.

Many dealers don't like buying trips because of the expense, the inconvenience, and the risk of coming home empty handed. I, however, cannot resist the promise of a deal anymore than a young man can resist the smile of a winsome young lady. And like a flirtatious smile that sets your heart afire, a phone call from a thousand miles away often proves too compelling to ignore, and you rush off, infatuated by the possibilities.

You know you're hooked when, even after experience has taught that nine times out of ten reality does not measure up to anticipation, you leave on a moment's notice, drive hundreds or fly thousands of miles in pursuit of the philatelic treasure at the end of the rainbow.

The other reason I follow leads is that I like to travel, especially in America's empty quarter: Wyoming, Montana, New Mexico, Arizona, Nevada, Utah. There's something about this land and being alone in a car on a perfect day with miles of straight road ahead that I cannot say no to. Maybe it's a feeling of kinship with the pioneers. Stamp dealers tend, by nature, to be rugged individualists.

For me the great American outback is a special land. A land of intense turquoise skies, red-tailed hawks soaring on unseen shafts of warm air, and towering, bleached-white, afternoon thunderheads. A land of limitless plains, ancient deserts, and ageless strata painted in broad, earthy, red, orange, and violet brush strokes. A land of arroyos, mesas, and cañons, of sagebrush, tumbleweed, and cactus. A land of isolated dwellings, solitary windmills, and weathered split-rail fences. A land where shimmering mirages float above 130° blacktop and billboards, faded pastel by perpetual sunshine, warn "Next Gas—60 Miles" and promise hot coffee and ice-cold beer.

It's a land of rough-at-the-edges, idiosyncratic souls: cowboys, desert rats, and truckstop waitresses named Laverne. A land of blue jeans, cowboy boots, and pickup trucks. A land whose anthems are sung by Johnny Cash and Patsy Cline. A land of open roads and uncluttered horizons. It's truly a land I cannot say no to.

Intellectually, you tell yourself you're on the road to expand your market and take advantage of buying opportunities. But in your heart, you know it's because you possess an unquenchable zest for deals, an adventurer's love of travel. Every stamp show beckons, like the sea whispers to the sailor, and every buying trip holds out the promise of treasure. You go because it's in your veins. You go because you have no choice.

Chapter 3

The time for stamp shows was during the boom of the late 1970s. The market churned like a cloudburst-swollen river. It teemed with buyers who chased deals with the frantic urgency of salmon running upstream. The market was so hot in those days that catalogues couldn't keep up. They were out of date before they were released.

Dealer advertisements offered to buy at 75-100 per cent of catalogue, even more for certain stamps. And stamps sold as quickly as they came in—at healthy markups. Dealers could afford to be generous because even if they overpaid, the rising tide of the market would lift them gently off the shoals in weeks, months at most.

Burgeoning prices created a free-for-all atmosphere that attracted scores of new dealers. Stamp dealers who only a short time before had been florists or dry cleaners or even Las Vegas blackjack dealers suddenly became experts on stamps and stamp investment. Bourse floors buzzed with investment talk. In that kaleidoscopic atmosphere of insatiable demand, new dealers found it possible to make money without even trying.

Stamp shows expanded until they could accommodate no more dealers. Waiting lists became the rule of the day. At every show, stories circulated about fabulous, astonishing deals. In a typical, but not unrealistic, story, Dealer A buys a collection on the floor of the show for $3,000, turns it over to Dealer B for $3,500, who turns over to Dealer C for $4,000, and so on until Dealer X pays $9,000 for it, then offers it back to Dealer A for $10,000 later the same day. Incredible as it sounds, those kinds of deals happened. Fortune whispered in everyone's ear, and it seemed that the only way you could lose was by not getting in on the action.

During the boom, I enjoyed meeting new dealers and learning about their backgrounds. Cal Carrson was a newcomer who, before getting into the stamp business, had dealt cards in Reno, Nevada. Cal was a natural salesman. I can't remember ever seeing him without an ear-to-ear, bright-as-a-sunny-morning smile. Cal dressed expensively, looked like he worked at a bank or stock brokerage.

"Used to deal a little blackjack, but mostly poker," Cal told me. "You think stamp shows are wild, you ought to spend some time in Reno at the poker tables."

"I'm afraid I'm not much of a poker player," I said, "and I've never played poker at a casino."

"Don't."

"How come? I thought the games were honest, that casinos made too much money to risk cheating."

"They don't exactly cheat, but they like to have the odds in their favor."

I raised my eyebrows. He'd lost me. "What do you mean by that?"

"If you've got six people at a poker table and five of them are playing for the house, you're not really cheating, just insuring that most hands will be won by the house. Law of averages, that's all. I've seen more than one guy bled dry that way."

"Oh," I said lamely.

Before we could continue our conversation, a shopper paused at his booth.

"Yes, sir," Cal said, flashing his sunny smile, "What can I help you with? Something for your collection? Or investment perhaps?"

"Kinda keeping my eye open for investment grade material," the shopper said, eyeing Cal's display.

"Wise strategy, indeed. I can tell you're a shrewd man," Cal said, tossing out the compliment as if it were a free sample.

"What do you recommend for investment?" the shopper asked, looking up from the counter display, warming to the flattery.

"Superb U.S. Top quality material has outperformed every other asset over the last decade. Here, have a seat. Make yourself comfortable. I've got some gorgeous material . . . material a man such as yourself will appreciate . . . at very smart prices."

The shopper sat down and listened attentively, unaware that the man he was asking for investment advice had been dealing cards in Reno only a few months before.

"See you later," I said, not wanting to intrude.

"Right," Cal said. "We'll get together for a drink or dinner sometime."

I walked back to my booth. In the hustle and bustle of the months that followed, we never did have that drink or dinner, and once the boom ended, Cal disappeared from the show circuit. I have no idea what happened to him.

If you attended bourses in those heady days, you remember hearing the cardinal selling points of philatelic investment repeated until everyone—dealer, collector and investor—accepted them as gospel.

Stamps were one of the few investments that did not lose value during the Depression. And it was true, but not for the reason everyone thought. Stamps were not objects of speculation in the 1920s, as were real estate and stocks. Stamps did not rise explosively in value, so there was no speculative bubble to burst. In the late 1970s, no one seemed to be aware of those facts. All they knew was that stamp values had not crashed during the Depression, implying there was no downside risk to stamp investment.

U.S. stamps have risen in value an average of 50 percent a year during the last five years. Again, it was true. But tangibles were the rage in those days: precious metals, gems, real estate, art. Economic newsletters stridently warned of hyperinflation and the coming collapse of paper-backed financial assets. Stamp collectors, aware of the great inflation that devastated Germany in the 1920s, when the cost to mail a letter rose from a few pfennigs to millions of marks in a relatively short time, took the warnings to heart.

I, too, worried about the destructive consequences of inflation. I, too, mistrusted financial assets. At the time, tangibles seemed like a safe haven for wealth. In retrospect, the mania seems a bit silly, but at the time, runaway inflation loomed as a very real threat. No one knew what lay ahead. If things had turned out a little differently, if inflation had swept the economy like wildfire, those who had bought tangibles would have made the smartest move of their lives.

Stamps have outperformed nearly every other tangible. Again, true, or so it seemed. I still question the reliability of price indexes for items such as old masters, Chinese ceramics, and stamps, because no objective means of recording and tracking transactions exists. In 1977, Salomon Brothers, a Wall Street brokerage firm, began issuing an annual report comparing long-term returns of selected financial and tangible assets. Stocks and bonds were at the bottom of the list. By 1979, stamps ranked fourth in performance during the previous decade with a compound rate of return of 15.4 percent. By comparison, stocks yielded only 2.9 percent and bonds, 6.1 percent. More startling were the gains during the preceding year, when stamps rose an astonishing 60.9 percent in value. By comparison, stocks were up a mere 5.3 percent, and bonds, 3.3 percent. Even gold trailed behind stamps, recording a 55 percent gain during the previous year.

Unfortunately, the stamp market interpreted the Salomon Brothers' report as an endorsement of the merits of stamps as investments. Salomon Brothers, however, dealt in financial assets, not tangibles. They issued the report to show investors that financial assets were undervalued and good bets for future gains.

The stamp market was oblivious to Salomon Brothers' motives. Stamp dealers, citing Salomon Brothers, touted stamps with the fervor of crusaders on a mission to the Holy Land. Stamp buyers regarded the report as recognition by Wall Street that stamps had become legitimate investments, and they bought, bought, bought.

In retrospect, Salomon Brothers was right. The late 1970s *was* the time to buy financial assets. During the 1980s, stocks soared, and tangibles nosedived. But who knew it then?

Stamps are highly portable and easily concealed. Those words struck a chord in a season rife with vague fears about everything from intrusive tax authorities to a currency collapse. Investors worried about the vulnerability of their assets. The fact that stamps are portable and easily concealable appealed to their sense of paranoia.

In reality, stamp prices soared because everyone wanted to buy and no one wanted to sell—and for no other reason. Bourses, like old-fashioned, gold-rush boom towns, swelled with eager new faces, guys you had never even heard of a year before. Neophyte dealers found it easy to sell. All they had to do was put their stamps out, and if collectors didn't snap them up, other dealers would. In no time at all, their pockets bulged with $100 bills.

The *nouveau riche* of the stamp trade hailed from many walks of life and dressed in everything from custom tailored three-piece suits to off-the-rack leisure suits. They popped champagne and picked up $500 dinner tabs as if they were nothing. They attended—and threw—lavish receptions and cocktail parties, Gatsbyesque affairs that effervesced with laughter and seemed to go on all night long. They mingled and joked and often made deals amounting to tens of thousands of dollars almost by accident. They ate and drank and spent money as if there were no tomorrow. And when morning came, it's a wonder any of them felt like showing up at the bourse. But they did, and the frenzied buying and selling went on and on and on.

Dealers, wearing satisfied smiles, scurried from table to table with deals tucked under their arms. Vestpocket dealers, satcheleers, and suitcase operators roamed show floors like rangeland coyotes, noses keen for the sweet scent of action. Banned from many shows, they—like coyotes—had a way of prospering despite fierce persecution.

European dealers, for whom dignity, style, and culture count so dearly, seemed out of place at those wild, free-for-all bourses. They held court in their booths, dressed in conservative suits and crisp, starched shirts, somewhat awestruck by the orgy of buying and selling going on around them. They seemed aloof, but I think they were simply self-conscious. They weren't used to the unrestrained enthusiasm of the American marketplace. They had arrived in the land of *Let's Make a Deal* where anybody could play, and they didn't know what to make of it.

Walking around bourse floors in those days, I felt like a stranger in a strange land.

"Caviar, Steve?" Bill Pickles asked as I passed his booth, offering me a thin wafer loaded with shiny black beads, as if to say, "Doesn't everyone snack on caviar in the afternoon?"

At another booth I overheard two dealers: "Flip you double or nothing. It's only two grand." And they flipped to settle the price of a deal.

"We gotta go," a young man in the purple velvet dinner jacket said to a young woman in low-cut, white evening gown, "The limo's waiting." He wore diamond cufflinks and a gold chain around his neck. She wore a ruby-colored necklace that harmonized perfectly with his dinner jacket. She took his arm, and they glided off to the limousine.

The market was swollen with newcomers who thought themselves dealers, but their lack of knowledge was often woefully obvious. Some overpriced their stamps, others underpriced them, and many displayed stamps that had been regummed or reperforated, unaware of the defects. And the market was oblivious to the incongruencies; everything sold. Everyone was happy.

The boom years were great. The euphoria seemed like it would last forever, but it didn't. The market turned in 1980. Gold and silver peaked and plummeted. Stamps—the depression-proof commodity—peaked and started sliding. By 1981 the economy was in recession, and the great stamp boom of the 1970s was history.

The market didn't bust overnight. The transition was more gradual, like warm summer days yielding to fall, then winter. Shows that once produced big crowds and abundant cash suddenly turned lackluster. At first, dealers blamed show promoters for poor publicity and promotion. Some even blamed cities, with comments such as "Bigsburgh just isn't a stamp town," and vowed not to return. They didn't realize the party was over. During the next few years, dealer ranks thinned by as much as 50 percent. Investment money dried up. Stamp prices fell. Stamp shows shrank. Waiting lists evaporated. And the myths—including the most dearly held, that stamps are depression proof—were shattered forever.

But it had been one hell of a party while it lasted!

Chapter 4

The boom of the late 1970s and early 1980s was an unforgettable time for dealers on the show circuit. Wild, celebratory nights-on-the-town followed frenetic days of non-stop wheeling and dealing.

There was the evening three of us dined at Spago, the well-known Los Angeles gathering spot for movie stars and celebrities. One of our party—I'll call him Trudeau—hailed from Canada. No sooner had we been seated than he produced a metal case from inside his jacket and offered us a hand-rolled Cuban cigar, considered contraband in the United States at that time. The quality of Havana cigars is legendary, so, although I'm not a smoker, I took one and lit up, just to see if they were as good as they were cracked up to be. We puffed our smokes and perused a menu of exotic entrees such as black angel hair pasta with goat cheese.

At one point, Trudeau said, "Isn't that Sally Field?" Then, "I've got to meet her." He jumped up and went to her table, while my other friend and I watched. She looked mildly annoyed, but the irrepressible Trudeau didn't seem to notice. He kept talking, and I wondered if he would offer her a cigar.

"Boy, what a great lady," he said, returning to our table.

A few minutes later, he said, "Isn't that what's-his-name?" I didn't know who he was talking about. "C'mon guys, help me out. What's that guy's name?"

"I don't know," I said. "I don't think these celebrities like being pestered." I was afraid he'd jump up and introduce himself to everyone in the restaurant.

"They don't mind," Trudeau said. "It's part of being famous. It's a big ego trip. They love it." He craned his neck, trying to see if he could spot other celebrities. Finally, we convinced him to remain seated and not make a spectacle of himself.

It was dark when we left Spago. A dozen *paparazzi* waited near the entrance for celebrities. They ignored us as we walked by. A few steps past them, Trudeau said loudly, "Great! They didn't recognize us." The *paparazzi* turned on us like a pack of wolves and gave chase, flashbulbs blazing. We ran to the car and waited helplessly for the doors to be unlocked while they battered us with photo flashes.

"Trudeau, you're impossible!" I cried as we jumped into the car.

"Those poor guys," he said, laughing, trying to catch his breath. "It's going to drive 'em nuts trying to figure out who we are!"

And there was the night Houston dealer Bob Dumaine treated me to his own special brand of Texas hospitality. It was closing time at a Dallas show. Eight of us planned to have dinner together. We'd agreed to meet in front of Bob's booth.

When I arrived, Bob and Eliot Warfield were engaged in a rapid-fire game of liar's poker at twenty dollars a shot. They rattled numbers back and forth, and at the end of each round, Bob scooped up another of Eliot's twenty-dollar bills. Eliot was down five or six hundred dollars but didn't seem to mind. Business had been good and cash flowed like oil from a West Texas gusher.

When our group had assembled, we left the bourse, walked through the hotel lobby and out the front entrance. Bob led the party, looking every bit the prosperous Texan: white Stetson, rawhide-colored suede sports coat, designer silk shirt, and alligator cowboy boots.

"Looks like we'll need a couple cabs," I said. Eight of us were too many for a single automobile.

"Hold on, Steve," Bob said, approaching the young man who had just parked the hotel's airport shuttle.

"Can you take us to Burrito Grande?" Bob asked him.

"Sorry, just to and from the airport," the young man replied.

"Gee, I was really hoping you could help us out," Bob said, holding a crisp $100 bill in front of the young man's face.

The youth did a double take, looked at the $100 bill, then stammered, "Wait a minute—I gotta clear this with the boss."

"Don't take too long," Bob advised. "We're kinda hungry."

"Be right back," he said, racing into the hotel.

"We could get a couple cabs for about twenty bucks," I said to Bob. "No use blowing a C-note."

"It's not my money," he said loudly. "It's Eliot's." Bob grinned, and Eliot returned the grin with a forced, sportsmanlike kind of smile.

The young shuttle driver dashed back and said, "Okay, but we gotta make it quick."

"All aboard," Bob announced. "Our buddy here's going to drive us to the restaurant."

Ten minutes later, we pulled up at Burrito Grande and piled out of the van. Bob, the last one out, holding the $100 bill in front of the young driver, tore it in half. He handed him half, saying, "Be back here at eleven, and you'll get the other half."

"Yes, sir!" the driver said.

Our party, Bob in the lead, surged into Burrito Grande like a dust devil on a hot summer day. The hostess seated us at a large circular table toward the rear of the restaurant.

"Drinks before dinner?" our waitress asked.

"You bet," Bob said. "Margaritas all around!"

"Eight margaritas," the waitress repeated, jotting the order on her pad.

"Eight *pitchers* of margaritas," Bob corrected, relishing the look of surprise on her face—and ours. I didn't think anyone could drink a whole pitcher of margaritas. I knew I couldn't. But no one objected. Rather, we were somehow pleased by the sheer extravagance of it.

"Eight pitchers of margaritas," the waitress said, noting the correction on her pad.

Soon three waitresses arrived laden with brimming pitchers of milky green liquid. They set one in front of each of us, giving the table a strange, top-heavy appearance.

"Here's a little something for your trouble," Bob said, handing our waitress a twenty-dollar bill.

"Thank you, sir," she drawled in a Texas accent as sweet and smooth as warm honey.

"Enjoy!" Bob said, raising his glass in a toast. Glasses clinked and we drank.

"I've heard of Texas hospitality—but eight pitchers of margaritas? Whew!" someone said.

"It's on Eliot," Bob said, in mock modesty, raising his glass to Eliot, who sat next to him. "Eliot's teaching me how to play liar's poker." We chuckled.

"I let him win," Eliot retorted, "To boost his ego."

We chuckled again.

Margaritas flowed. The banter and laughter grew louder as the level of green liquid in the pitchers fell. Bob and Eliot traded quips continuously.

Diners at other tables discreetly craned their necks to see what was going on. Like an owl perched in the shadows of a tall pine, the restaurant manager kept a watchful eye on us from the distant foyer, probably wishing we'd leave.

"Are you ready to order?" our waitress asked at length. If she hadn't reminded us, we would have forgotten about eating altogether. We placed our orders and soon the food arrived.

The banter continued, but neither Bob nor Eliot gained the upper hand in their ongoing game of one-upmanship. Then Eliot slipped a rib bone, sticky with barbecue sauce, into the lower pocket of Bob's suede jacket. Bob remained unaware of the rib for some time, until, with a little prompting from Eliot, he reached into his pocket.

His hand touched the cold, slimy bone, and a look of amazement crossed his face. He turned to Eliot, as if to say *"Whaaaat?"* He pulled the bone out of his pocket, holding it gingerly between his thumb and forefinger as if it were a dead rat. It left ugly streaks of sticky reddish-brown barbecue sauce on the suede, streaks that even the most expert dry cleaner would be hard pressed to get out.

A laughing demon seized Eliot. The rest of us watched silently.

"Hey, this isn't *New York* suede, Eliot," Bob cried. "Fun's fun, but there's a limit!"

"Jeez, I thought you'd take it as a joke," Eliot said when the laughing demon had left him.

"This jacket cost a lot of money, and I didn't win that much from you!" Bob said, wiping at the gooey streaks.

Bob was not amused; clearly, things had gone too far. Our table grew subdued.

At eleven, we trooped out. The hotel van was waiting for us. Bob, the last one aboard, handed the young driver the other half of the $100 bill and said, "Home, James."

"Yes, sir!" the driver said, and we sped off toward the hotel.

The way Bob tells it, the story didn't end that night. He saved the offending barbecued rib, took it home, and froze it. It remained comatose in his freezer for several years.

Then, in response to a wedding invitation from Eliot, Bob Federal Expressed the frozen bone to him as a wedding gift. According to Bob, Eliot opened the gift in front of the assembled guests at his wedding reception. Out came the cold, sticky rib. An embarrassed Eliot, holding the messy bone, could offer no explanation for the bizarre gift.

Only later, when Bob reminded him of the night in Dallas several years earlier, did Eliot understand the motive behind the gift and appreciate the humor of it. They laughed once again. It had been a good time, one the of the more memorable evenings of the glory years.

Chapter 5

Nights out after a show are fun, but first you've got to get there. Getting there—that's the nuts and bolts of being on the road. And one who's on the road week in and week out soon discovers that travel is not as glamorous as it sounds. I got to the point after the first year or so where I hated airports. To this day, I'd rather spend ten hours driving than six or eight hours hustling to an airport, waiting for a flight, sitting jammed into an uncomfortable seat, then hassling with baggage claim and ground transportation.

Despite its discomforts, air travel is often the most efficient way to get where you need to go. I learned that smart dealers always arrive early at airports. I've seen grown men throw temper tantrums because they were bumped from a flight for arriving a few minutes late.

I learned that smart dealers always take direct flights—even if the hours are inconvenient. Tales of missed connections are legion. Impromptu changes in plan are the last thing you need when trying to keep a tight schedule.

Doing stamp shows is an exercise in logistics. You pack your stock carefully in sturdy cases, making every cubic inch count. You lock your cases and check them as baggage. Every time my stock disappears on an airport conveyor, I wonder if I'm ever going to see it again. Murphy's law, "Anything that can go wrong, will go wrong," lurks in the back of my mind. I've heard too many horror stories from fellow dealers about lost luggage and sleepless nights waiting for missing stock to turn up. Only when familiar cases and trunks reappear at baggage claim does your anxiety subside.

After you've claimed your luggage, the next step is to move it to the show. If you're lucky, the show is near the airport, and you get a free ride in the hotel shuttle. If not, you take a cab or rent a car. If you're smart, you arranged to arrive either before or after rush hour. There's nothing worse than watching a cab's meter run faster than the cab itself moves.

Hotels don't always record reservations correctly. More than once I've faced a hotel clerk who has said: "Datz? Sorry, no record of a reservation under that name."

It's a terrible, helpless, sinking feeling to hear that after a long day on the road, your baggage and show stock piled high on a bellman's cart behind you.

"But I've got a confirmation number." I rummage through my pockets to find the magic number. "Yes, here it is—SS-409409."

Computer keys click. The clerk tries to resurrect the missing reservation. "You sure it was for today?" she asks in a doubtful tone.

"Yes."

More clicking keys, then, "No, it's not here, sorry. And we're booked solid—we've got a stamp convention and a dentists' convention," she says with an air of finality.

"I'm with the stamp convention," I explain. "That's why I have to have a room here. I made a reservation," I insist. "I've got a confirmation number."

I will not be dissuaded, so the clerk waves for the manager. He hurries over, looks concerned, listens, nods sympathetically.

I'm adamant. I was up at dawn, fought rush hour traffic to get to the airport, parked in the outlying parking and walked forever to get to the terminal, waited 45 minutes because my flight was late, worried about my stock getting lost, spent $30 to sit in a filthy cab, only to be told I don't have a room. I stab at the confirmation number with my finger, trying not to become more agitated.

"Just a moment," the manager says, taking the confirmation number and clicking away at the computer terminal. His hair is neatly combed, his shirt pressed, his tie straight. His blue blazer looks like it just came off the rack. My hair is windblown, my shirt feels sticky, my tie is loose, and my sports coat is rumpled. I feel as if I've been wearing the same clothes for three days. I want to get my stock to the bourse, secure it, go to my room, take a shower, and relax for a while.

"We do have a reservation for you, Mr. Datz," the manager says. "Three nights, checking in November nineteenth."

"November *nineteenth?*" I exclaim. "I made the reservation for today—November ninth—not the nineteenth. I'm with the stamp show. Why would I make a reservation for the nineteenth?"

The manager shrugs. "Perhaps you made a mistake," he says, then mindful of the look on my face, "Or perhaps the reservation clerk misunderstood."

"I didn't make a mistake," I assert. "I'm very careful. I've had problems like this before, and that's precisely why I'm so careful. I'm here for the stamp show. Look at that baggage." I point to the bellman's cart loaded with cartons and cases. "I need a room here—*today!*"

"Okay, okay," the manager says, "let's see if we can help you." He huddles with the clerk, then punches a few computer keys, waits, punches a few more. "Okay, we've found a room for you," he says, and instructs the clerk to register me.

I breathe a sigh of relief. At least I won't have to stay in a miles-distant hotel. There have been times when there was no room, no sympathetic manager, and I've ended up across town. The clerk hands me a registration form to sign, and my anger gives way to road-weariness.

"Thank you very much," I say. "I really appreciate it."

"That's what we're here for," the manager replies cheerfully.

I am well aware that the manager has given me a room knowing there are always a few no-shows. I've arrived mid-afternoon while he still has plenty of leeway in his bookings. Had I arrived at ten o'clock at night, the extra rooms would be gone and I'd be staying somewhere else. *Yes,* I tell myself, *the smart dealer always arrives early.*

You hope the bourse room will have been set up by the time you arrive and that security is in place so that you can safely leave your stock. Sometimes, the room isn't set up, and you have to wait until late at night to move in.

You hope security is tight. Sometimes it's not, and you worry about leaving your stock. At a show a few years back, I ran into a vestpocket dealer on move-in night.

"Hi, Ralph," I said, eyeing his dealer badge, "I didn't know you had a table here."

"I don't."

"How did you get a badge?"

"The guy out front asked if I was a dealer, guest, judge, or volunteer. I told him dealer. He didn't ask if I had a table, just told me to sit down, snapped my picture, and handed me the badge."

I wasn't worried about Ralph, but the knowledge that almost anyone could get a badge made me vaguely distrustful of security at that show.

On move-in night at another show, they made a big fuss about everyone having a photo ID badge, but failed to post a guard at the front door to check who had badges and who didn't. Anyone could walk into the bourse.

Even if the bourse room is set up, lots of things can go wrong. Your location can be different than promised. The change can be unintentional, the result of poor planning, last minute additions, or cancellations.

A dealer's worst nightmare is, upon arriving, being informed that there is no record of his reserving or paying for a table. You're standing there dumbfounded, stock ready to move in, while the bourse chairman says, "We wondered why you weren't coming this year."

"But I paid in full—a couple of months ago!"

"Nope," he says, scanning his roster. "Don't show any record of it."

It's happened to me. And it's very disturbing, like one of those dreams where you show up at the office in your underwear. After being informed they had no record of my paying for a table, I stood there watching the other dealers set up, knowing I had sent payment in full, struggling to make sense of it, wondering what I would do. The bourse chairman asked me if I had a record of the payment, but I didn't. Who carries their cancelled checks with them?

To the bourse chairman's credit, rather than make an issue of it, he found space and set up tables for me. We agreed to settle the matter of the missing payment later, when we'd both had a chance to review our records. The moment I arrived home, I went to my check register. I *had* paid for the table—more than two months earlier. Riffling through my bank statements, however, I discovered the check had never been cashed. Had it been lost in the mail or misplaced by the show committee? To this day, we don't know. Fortunately, the bourse chairman accommodated me, I issued a replacement check, and everything turned out all right.

Sometimes—but not often—the whole show is poorly laid out. One show allowed only five feet of aisle space between tables. People couldn't move around without pressing against each other or bumping into those seated at bourse tables. The layout probably looked good on paper; too bad no one thought to test a mockup. Most shows allow ten to twelve feet for aisles, the minimum necessary for smooth traffic flow.

The amount of space between your front and back tables can vary from a cramped couple of feet to six or eight feet. When the tables are too close together, it's difficult to move around without constantly bumping into things. When they're too far apart, it's inconvenient to reach for stock or make change. It would be nice if there were a standard from show to show.

Your table can be the wrong size. The standard is eight feet long by thirty inches wide. Sometimes, you're provided with six foot tables or tables only eighteen inches wide. It's annoying—and unfair—to be confronted with tables smaller than you expected. You plan on a certain amount of space on which to display your stock and conduct business, and you need every inch of it.

Your booth can be configured incorrectly, a single instead of a double or a corner—or vice versa. The lighting may be lousy. The electric plugs may not work. The air conditioner may be right above you and continuously cascade cold air on you.

At one show, I made it past all the hurdles only to find that my metal cabinet didn't have a key. I went back to the registration table to find out who had the keys.

"I do," said a helpful volunteer, tossing me a set.

"But you don't even know which booth I'm in," I said.

"Doesn't matter. They're all the same."

I didn't bother to ask what good a locking cabinet was if everyone had the same keys. I walked away in disgust, thinking whoever planned security for that show was dull-witted.

Sometimes, your cabinet's lock doesn't work. Or the cabinet is slightly bent so that the adjustable shelves can't be rearranged or even set up. Or your booth is set up but the cabinet hasn't arrived.

Sometimes, instead of being able to move in right away, you encounter a large, vacant, echoey hall with stacks of plywood-topped tables, piles of yet-to-be-hung drapery, and a confused foreman wandering around, blueprint in hand, trying to make sense of the layout.

Worse yet, sometimes the bourse chairman can't be located to register a complaint. There should be a rule that bourse chairmen remain on site during setup.

Even when the bourse room is ready, there are times when you cannot go right in. Sometimes, you run afoul of union rules, such as having to have a union man assist if you need to use a wheeled cart. Then, it seems as if you must wait forever. In the interests of expediency, you flag down the union steward and slip him ten or twenty bucks, then, magically, your stock is moved in right away. No, it doesn't seem fair, but you come to regard it as just another operating expense.

Sometimes, you have to schlep cases yourself. Bob Dumaine once remarked that he'd gone from a size 33 sleeve length to a size 35 as a result of schlepping stock in and out of shows. I'm still not sure whether he was joking.

You learn to make sure your room is never above, below or next to a hospitality suite. After spending a long day on the road, nothing makes life more miserable than being kept awake until the wee hours by a bunch of loud revelers.

Finally, having survived the rigors of the journey, you fall back on your pillow and try to get some sleep. Tomorrow will be a busy day.

Chapter 6

In the morning, you detail your booth, prepare to greet customers and do business. Often, however, the first man you meet is not a customer, but the tax man. They gather from city, county, state, and even regional jurisdictions, like flies attracted to a honey pot. They come laden with triplicate forms and sheaves of regulations. Some are courteous, others are not. The moment they hand you forms, you grab for your wallet because you've learned to expect the worst. You're usually required to cough up $10-$25 for the license, then collect the appropriate sales tax. Typically, you settle up at the close of the show or mail in your payment—that's in benevolent jurisdictions.

No-so-benevolent jurisdictions go for the throat. Their license fees are higher, and they demand a deposit. One southern California city requires a deposit of one hundred dollars in *cash* against taxes collected. And they don't refund the unused portion of the deposit at the end of the show. You've got to file paperwork and wait weeks before you see a refund. They understand the principle of operating on other people's money. Posting deposits might not sound like a big deal, but if every city required a $100 deposit, you could easily have a substantial amount of capital tied up waiting for refunds. I prefer not to do business that way, so I don't do shows in that city.

Most jurisdictions aren't so demanding, and most tax agents are pleasant and easy to work with—but not all. At one combination coin-and-stamp show, the tax man strutted from booth to booth pompously reciting the rules in a quintessential performance of bureaucratic pettiness. The stamp dealers grumbled, but quietly signed up. The coin dealers, however, were cut from different cloth—they raised hell!

"You damn guys ought to be out fixing potholes or doing something constructive, instead of hassling us dealers!" one angry coin dealer thundered. His voice could be heard all over the bourse. The tax man must have been all bark and no bite because he just stood there and took it. The other dealers followed the first dealer's lead, and, before the morning was over, the luckless revenuer suffered verbal abuse from dozens of ill-tempered coin dealers. Finally, he retreated to the lobby, tail between his legs. The bourse filled with laughter when he announced over the public address system that dealers could register at a table he'd set up in the lobby.

Dealers don't like being hassled by tax men nor do collectors like being asked for sales tax, especially on large purchases.

"I've gotta pay sales tax on this?" the customer asks, as if I'm trying to cheat him, as if I get to keep the tax money. "None of the other dealers are charging tax."

"Sorry, I didn't make the laws. I'm just trying to obey them."

"Hmmph," the annoyed buyer snorts. After purchasing several hundred dollars worth of stamps, he's in no mood to see another seven percent added to the total.

"Did it ever occur to you that I don't enjoy collecting sales tax? Why don't you complain to the legislature? They're the ones who passed the law," I remark, and I'm serious. Stamp dealers don't enact sales tax laws, and they get tired of being blamed for having to collect taxes.

Colorado, my home state, is becoming overzealous in its sales tax rules. In-state dealers, like all merchants, are required to have a regular sales tax license. Dealers who go to shows must have a "special events" license. There is a special events license for events with three or more vendors and another license for events with less than three vendors. So, if you have a retail location, do shows, and conduct an off-premises auction, you are required to have three separate licenses to collect the same state sales tax.

"Hell, civilization won't end in a nuclear war—it'll suffocate under all this damn bureaucracy," one coin dealer, who resembled a cross between a grizzly bear and the Pillsbury doughboy, griped. When I first heard the remark, I thought it sounded melodramatic. I'm not so sure anymore.

In any case, when the show finally opens, you greet customers, listen to requests, and try to accommodate them, or, if you can't, direct them to someone who can. Most customers are cheerful, reasonable, rational people, the kind you enjoy helping. In fact, one thoughtful customer always brings me a pastry or insists on treating me to a soft drink. You don't forget those small kindnesses.

One of the nicest things about the stamp business is the people. They share information about their specialties, and you reciprocate. Their purchases pay your expenses and provide your profit. And, when the day is over, you leave the show weary but satisfied that it's been worth all the effort.

Chapter 7

NOSHOWPEX is generic terminology for a poorly attended show. There were more and more of them after 1980 when the stamp market headed south. But like troupers, many dealers continued to do the show circuit, confident the recession would be short and that the market would quickly rebound.

I attended one NOSHOWPEX in the early 1980s where customers were as scarce as palm trees in Siberia. The sponsoring group had done a good job. The ballroom was spacious and well laid out. Exhibits were first class. The show just happened to be in a city with few collectors. The bourse was dead Friday. Dealers spent the day perusing one another's stocks, hoping Saturday would be better. Unfortunately, it was not. A dozen or so attendees wandered the thirty-dealer bourse, moving from table to table with tantalizing slowness.

"Talk about the walking dead," Bill Pickles said from the booth next to mine. It was the same Bill Pickles who'd offered me caviar only a couple years earlier. Boy, how times had changed! Bill and I played gin rummy to pass the hours and traded stories about the slowest shows we'd ever attended. We debated where to go for dinner that evening, and wondered aloud if we'd make show expenses. Occasionally, we glanced up from our cards hoping one of the attendees was headed our way, but they always hovered a row or two away, their faces—it seemed—as vacant as the bourse itself.

Action breeds action. At a busy show, everyone wants a seat, no one wants to miss out on a deal, no one wants the fellow ahead of him to get the treasure before he's had a chance. When your table's busy, everyone wants in on the action. When it's dead, nothing works to attract customers.

Most of the tables at NOSHOWPEX were deserted. The room reminded me of a mouth agape in a long, bored yawn. Dealers prowled each other's tables reflexively, looking for something to buy, but the best material had changed hands the day before.

As we played cards, an older gentleman walked up to my table and asked enthusiastically, "Are you from Denver? They told me out front that there was a dealer from Denver here."

"Yes, I'm from Denver."

"Great! I was hoping to find someone from Colorado. I've got something to show you. Only someone from Colorado could appreciate this," he said, pulling a black binder from his attaché case and handing it to me.

I opened it. It was a collection of Colorado viewcards, hotel baggage labels, and paper ephemera. Many of the cards featured views of early Colorado mining towns such as Central City, Leadville, and Aspen. The binder also contained quite a few cards depicting steam engines and trains. The colorful baggage labels dated from the 1920s and 1930s and included well-known hotels such as the Brown Palace in Denver and the Broadmoor in Colorado Springs.

I didn't have the foggiest notion of what I'd do with it. Besides, the owner was so excited I was sure he would want a fortune for it. I didn't even want to ask how much.

"Unusual items," I said. "But I'm not sure I'm the right guy for the collection. It's really not philatelic. I have no idea what it's worth."

"I want twenty-five bucks for it," he replied without hesitation. "It's not doing me any good, so if you're willing to give twenty-five dollars for it, it's yours."

"Okay," I said, surprised at his price, but thinking I couldn't go wrong for $25. I figured I'd offer it in my next auction, where I thought it might bring $50, perhaps a little more. I had no idea it would turn out to the bright spot of the show.

I wrote the man a check, which he folded carefully and put in his shirt pocket. Then, he wandered off to browse at the other tables. Bill and I returned to our card game, which stretched on with few interruptions until, mercifully, it was time to close.

Back in Denver, I had forgotten about the collection, until a dealer—who I'll call Rollo Worthington—breezed into my office.

"What's new?" he asked. "Bring anything back from NO-SHOWPEX?"

As soon as I saw Rollo, I thought of the collection. Rollo was a first-rate wheeler-dealer with an indestructible air of self-confidence and the killer instinct of a tiger. Rollo wasn't mean-spirited or unpleasant, he just charged the maximum the traffic would bear.

Rollo's style intrigued me. He was charming, and there was something daring and decisive about the way he operated. At the same time, I was wary of him because every time we did business, I came off second best.

Once, when Rollo had asked the fateful question, "What's new?" I'd answered too hastily, perhaps unconsciously hoping to impress him. "Just got a tremendous Zeppelin cover in," I said.

He looked it over quickly, then came right to the point. "Can you let me have it for twenty-four hours? I think I've got someone for it."

I hesitated because I, too, had a customer for it.

"Twenty-four hours," he pressed. "One day."

"I want six hundred for it," I said, hoping the price would deflect his interest. I'd planned to ask $650 retail for the cover, which I thought was reasonable.

"No problem," Rollo said, indifferent to the price. He liked covers, especially scarce covers, because little existed in the way of pricing guides, which allowed him big profits.

I sighed silently, then said, "Okay. If you have a customer for it, go ahead and take it. But if you're planning to beat the bushes, forget it. I've got my own potential customer, and I don't want the cover shopped around."

"No problem," Rollo said, looking pained that I'd suggest such a thing.

I let him take the cover because $600 was only slightly less than I'd planned to ask, and, besides, my customer might well pass.

The next morning, my phone rang. The caller was the very man I had had in mind for the cover.

"I need some advice, Steve. I've just been offered a very scarce Zeppelin cover . . ."

Somehow, I knew it was the cover I had let Rollo take, and I was angry with myself for letting him take it.

". . . for seventeen hundred dollars. Do you think that's a good price?"

I just about choked. I wanted to shout *"Seventeen hundred dollars is an absolute, total rip-off!"* but held my tongue. No use jumping to conclusions.

"Can you describe the cover?"

"Sure," he replied, describing the cover I had lent Rollo.

"You could probably find one for less," I advised, trying to be diplomatic. "Seventeen hundred sounds a bit pricey."

"That's what I thought. Just wanted your opinion."

"Do you mind if I ask who offered you the cover?"

"I'd rather not say."

"I understand."

"Thanks for the advice." He hung up.

I was furious. Rollo had gone straight to my customer. After I calmed down, I realized I should have known better. It was my fault for letting him take the cover.

So, when Rollo walked into my office the day after I had returned from NOSHOWPEX and asked "What's new?" I immediately thought of the viewcard collection.

"I just picked this up," I said, tossing it casually on the desk.

Rollo liked history. I felt sure he would like the collection. He spent quite a while paging through it. Meanwhile, I debated about how much to ask for it, remembering all the times I'd come out on the short end.

"Nice," he allowed. "How much?"

"Five hundred," I said, picking a number out of thin air.

Rollo frowned, something he rarely did. The frown remained as he paged through the collection a second time, deep in deliberation. He wanted it, but the price bothered him. I had never seen him so perplexed. Admittedly, the price was punitive, but I was tired of being on the receiving end. If he wanted it, he'd have to pay the price.

"Three hundred," he countered, still frowning.

"Sorry, the price is five hundred," I said coolly.

"Where do you get a price like that? I don't think it's worth five hundred."

"You have to ask yourself, 'When was the last time I saw a collection like this? When will I ever see another?'"

Rollo struggled with the dilemma, looking uncharacteristically grim. I was sure he'd pass.

Then, he said, "Okay. It's more than I ought to pay, but you're right. Who knows when I'll ever see another."

The viewcard collection helped me recoup some of my expenses for NOSHOWPEX. But, even with the price I had extracted from Rollo, the show hadn't paid for itself.

The recession of 1981 stripped the market of investors and Johnnie-come-lately dealers, the sources of cash that had fueled the hurricane of the boom. Shows seemed slow and discouraging. Crowds were thinner, sales smaller, profits leaner. Half the dealers doing the show circuit during the boom left the business—simply disappeared. Travel was less profitable, and only the strong survived.

During the boom, it was common to hear dealers boast about how well they were doing. The comments went something like this: "It's been a great show. Just bought a deal for twenty grand and flipped it half an hour later for twenty-two."

"Bought a set of Zepp plates this morning and sold it to an investor this afternoon—made a quick ten grand!"

"Made three grand by just walking this collection across the room!"

In the halcyon days, no one regarded those kinds of comments as boasts. Everyone seemed to be making big deals, and the stories were offered more in a tone of disbelief than of bragging. Dealers were simply amazed at how easy it was to make money.

But that all changed after the boom. The big deals and instant cash disappeared. The object was to make expenses and, with luck, show a profit.

"How's your show?" was no longer an invitation to share one's incredible experiences. Instead, one hoped to hear, "Almost cleared expenses. If the rest of the day is decent and there's any activity tomorrow, I'll do okay."

One expected bad news. Hearing bad news had a comforting effect; it confirmed that business was slow for everyone. It was a relief to hear that others were as pinched as you were. After the boom, dealers acquired a certain humility. At least, most did.

At a particularly slow show, I passed one of the show circuit regulars on my way back from the restroom. I greeted him with the usual "How's your show?"

"Not too great," he said, "I've only done fifty thousand so far."

Only fifty thousand! Was the man serious? I had taken in only $3,000 and found it impossible to believe anyone could have taken in $50,000, or, if they had, that they would complain the show was *not too great.*

"How's your show?" he asked.

I was tempted to say, "Lousy, I've only done a hundred grand." Instead, I said, "It's been pretty fair," trying to sound upbeat.

"Maybe things will pick up," he said, strolling on down the aisle. Was he joking? I couldn't decide. The only thing that came to mind was the old saying Texas dealer Bob Dumaine is so fond of: "An empty barrel makes the loudest noise."

Sometimes, shows are slow because of their geographical location. Small towns just don't have the collector base to pull big crowds. It's not the fault of the organizers, and they're usually unaware of the problem. But it's apparent to dealers who travel extensively and are used to the bustling crowds at major shows.

At one slow local show, it seemed that everyone looked at the stamps at my table but moved on without buying.

J.B., my assistant, remarked, "This crowd's so slow they wouldn't buy dollar bills for ninety-five cents."

The thought amused me. "I'll bet you're right," I said, taking a dollar bill and slipping it under the glass. I lettered a price tag and placed it below the bill: *Show Special, 95 cents.*

J.B. chuckled, and we waited. People drifted by, casually viewed our display, including the discounted dollar bill, and wandered off. We expected some reaction, but no one said a word.

After a few minutes, I reduced the price to 90 cents. "There," I said, "now maybe we'll get some action."

More time and more browsers passed, but nothing happened. So, I marked the dollar bill down to 85 cents, then 80 cents, then 75 cents.

"I'm going to mark it down until it sells," I said.

Half an hour later, still no action. It wasn't that passersby didn't see the bill. It was prominently displayed. They just ignored it! I knew that some of those browsers would argue tenaciously for a 10 or 15 percent discount on a stamp purchase. I couldn't understand why they wouldn't buy a dollar bill discounted 25 percent. The more time that passed, the more the situation amused us.

I thought I had a sale when one fellow asked, "Is that bill genuine?"

"Yes, sir," I answered.

But he just nodded and moved on.

"Can you believe it?" I asked J.B., who shook his head. "You'd think that people would snap up a dollar bill priced at seventy-five cents."

"Maybe they think it's a gimmick."

"But I just told the man it was genuine."

J.B. shrugged. It was baffling, but at least it dispelled the boredom. More than an hour had passed. During that time, I lowered the price again and again, until, finally, it was down to 50 cents. J.B. and I sat like two fishermen with lines in the water, watching trout everywhere and wondering why they wouldn't rise to the bait.

When we'd just about given up hope, an older gentlemen stopped and looked at the dollar bill for a long time.

"The price on that bill fifty cents?" he asked.

"That's right."

"What's wrong with it?"

"Nothing."

He looked skeptical.

"What's the catch?"

"No catch, but you've got to pay cash. No checks on currency purchases," I said. J.B. stifled a chuckle.

"Hmm. I guess I ought to take it then," he said, counting out a quarter, two dimes, and a nickel.

"Would you like a sack for it?" I asked, removing the dollar bill from under the plexiglass.

"No thanks, I'll just put it in here," he said, taking out his wallet. He tucked the bill into the wallet, slid it into his back pocket, and walked off without another word.

"Only took an hour and a half to move that bill," I said, looking at my watch.

"At least it moved. I was beginning to worry."

"Well, that's the kind of show it's been. At least, if anyone asks, I can say with a straight face that it was so slow you could barely sell dollar bills at half price."

And that's how it was after the boom ended.

Chapter 8

Stamp shows remind me of old-fashioned, fun-filled county fair carnivals. Collectors browse and spend more than they intend, justify their purchases with the thought that a price was just too good to pass up or an item so scarce it wouldn't likely be found again soon. Old acquaintanceships are renewed, new friends made, and latest acquisitions enthusiastically, if somewhat immodestly, shown off.

Anyone who has ever marveled at a well prepared philatelic exhibit has promised himself that someday his collection will be as well organized, coherent, and elegantly presented. The promise is made silently and with the solemn resolve of a New Year's resolution.

Beautifully manicured exhibits don't come easy. They are the product of months or years of careful preparation: mounting, remounting, researching and writing up a body of work that, hopefully, judges will look favorably upon. Exhibitors dream of gold medals, but dare not hope too much. When the show is over, some will have been pleasantly surprised, others disappointed.

Paul Ballard couldn't hide the disappointment in his voice the day he and I walked down the row of frames in which his collection was exhibited.

"I'd hoped for a gold," Paul said as we walked. "I really thought I had a shot at it this time. At least, I got a bronze."

"There's nothing wrong with a bronze," I said.

"I know, but we all dream of gold."

As we walked, Paul pointed out highlights.

"This postmark," he said, pointing to a brown-colored cover, "was used for only a couple of weeks right after the German invasion."

The cover looked ordinary, not something I would have recognized as rare and elusive. It could have come from a dealer's dollar box. One of the great things about philately is the knowledge you gain from it, and in the few minutes Paul and I walked through his exhibit, I learned a lot about the German invasion of Poland, Russia, and the eastern territories during World War II.

"Here are inscription blocks of the first occupation issue," Paul said. "The judges didn't like them. Told me I had too many stamps. 'Covers tell the story,' they said. 'Get more covers.'

"After every show, I go home and fine tune the exhibit again. My original intent was to form a specialized collection, but, more and more, I'm organizing the collection according to the suggestions of judges. And many items such as these inscription blocks—which are very scarce—are important to me, but not to the judges," Paul sighed.

Paul's exhibit looked good to me, but I'm not a philatelic judge. The pages were neatly typed, the text carefully placed, the material interesting and not commonly encountered. Paul had an eye for quality, a knack for finding scarce covers in choice condition. I appreciated what I saw.

"I'm getting tired of redoing pages," Paul said. "I take the time because I want to get it right—I want to get a gold. But every time I exhibit, there's always something more to do. Sometimes I wonder if I'll ever get it right."

Paul's exhibit contained more German occupation covers than I had ever seen in one place. Strolling down the aisle, reading snatches of translated correspondence, I began to empathize with the agonizing uncertainty dislocated families felt in that terrible time when Hitler's armies rolled across Europe. Did the family who received a card advising that the writer was in "protective custody" have any inkling that that euphemism meant he was being detained in a concentration camp? Another postcard, stamped *Konzentrationslager Auschwitz*, described the pleasant surroundings encountered by a newly arrived inmate and made everything sound disarmingly routine. A postcard from occupied Poland to an address in Hungary reported that the writer had had no word from Papa, but hoped to hear from him soon.

I found Paul's exhibit compelling.

"Success in exhibiting depends on many factors," I said. "Competition, for one. A gold medal exhibit in one show might earn only a silver or bronze in the next, depending on what it's up against. And despite the effort to be objective, judging contains an element of subjectivity, just like Olympic ice skating or diving. Not all judges see an exhibit the same way. Competition's fun, but sometimes you've just got to please yourself.

"I used to wonder if I was going about collecting right . . . until I saw a psychiatrist," I said.

Paul turned his head toward me, eyebrows raised.

"Oh, it's not what you think," I said, chuckling at his reaction. "I interviewed the man for an article. Over the years, I've spent quite a bit of time trying to figure out what stamp collecting's all about. And I'm not the only one, judging by the number of people who ask me how to go about it.

"It's possible to get a lot of mixed signals. 'How To' books point you in one direction. Your local club might point you in another. Experienced collectors tend to guide you in the direction they've taken. Stamp dealers share their ideas, which might point in yet another direction. Columnists in philatelic periodicals offer ideas on their approach to the hobby. There are so many different opinions, pretty soon you wonder where you're headed."

"Well, I started out as a general collector," Paul said. "Learned about the hobby along the way, narrowed my interest to a country, then a specialty, sought out quality material that I could afford, researched my specialty, and put together an exhibit."

"Exhibit," I echoed. "You said *exhibit,* not *collection.* I think you've defined your approach without realizing it. Your collection is an exhibit. That's what you enjoy. So, that's what you should do."

"What did the psychiatrist say?" Paul asked. "Are stamp collectors all nuts?"

"No," I chuckled, "But that's what the grouchy old clerk at the country post office where I used to buy stamps as a kid thought. I'd look up at him through the brass bars of his window, scared to death to ask for a plate block. 'Kids and fools,' he'd say sternly, looking down his nose at me, 'Only kids and fools collect stamps. You're still a kid, so I guess it's okay.' I'd push twelve cents across the counter, and he'd hand me a commemorative plate block with great condescension. 'Now run along, Sonny—you're keeping people with real business waiting.' So, for years I suspected that people who collect stamps were fools."

"Are they?"

"No, the psychiatrist put my mind at ease. He said stamp collecting is perfectly normal."

"Why *do* people collect?" Paul asked.

"For lots of reasons, according to the doctor. Some straightforward, others more obscure and deep-seated. The doctor said that human beings tend to be acquisitive. Some collect stamps, others coins or cars or matchbook covers—all kinds of things. It's human nature. For some people it's a hobby, for others a business or profession. The corporate empire builder may be driven by the same motivation that causes collectors to acquire stamps. They act on their impulses in different ways.

"He said that, as a hobby, collecting is therapeutic. Stamps take our minds off other problems, allow us to relax, give us time away from the stresses of everyday life.

"My approach to collecting is different from the way most people go about it. Interviewing the doctor made me realize there's no right or wrong way to collect. The way people collect reflects personality. The important thing is to enjoy it."

As Paul and I slowly strolled along the rows of exhibits, we continued chatting.

"This exhibit on the postal history was formed by someone with a keen interest in history. Perhaps he'd rather be a historian than whatever he does for a living. Researching, forming his collection gives him an outlet for that aspiration. Notice how much detail he's incorporated into the exhibit," I said, pointing to letters displayed with covers.

"And here's an artist," I said, pointing to another. "The stamps are common, but look how much trouble he's taken illustrating the pages. They looked like *illuminati* manuscripts.

"An aggressive personality gets pleasure from the hunt, the thrill of the chase. He quickly loses interest in a stamp once he's obtained it. Then there's the treasure hunter, the one who never seems to get around to mounting his stamps, but spends hours going through mystery lots searching for the elusive rarities. Some enjoy the give-and-take of haggling, the art of the deal. Others look at stamps as investments and dabble in them instead of stocks or bonds.

"That's the neat thing about stamps—you can do whatever pleases you."

"Maybe I wanted to be an Olympic athlete," Paul mused. "Maybe that's why I'm so gung-ho about exhibiting."

"Could be, but whatever the reason, the important thing is to do what you enjoy. That's what I do."

"What do you collect?" Paul asked.

"Whatever strikes my eye. No rhyme or reason to it. I like the artwork, especially the engraved look of stamps from the 1930s through the 1960s. To me, it was the golden era of stamp production. So, when I see a set or single that appeals to me, I grab it. I guess you could call it a topic—things I like. There's no pressure for completion, and I get a tremendous amount of enjoyment from the stamps I've accumulated.

"For many years, I took the traditional approach, filled spaces, worked toward completion. Then one day, I found myself debating whether to spend several hundred dollars for a nineteenth century stamp whose appearance I didn't particularly care for. In fact, it was downright ugly, but I needed it to fill a space. Finally, I said to myself, *Why should I spend so much money for a stamp I don't even like?* I couldn't think of a single reason, so I didn't buy it. Instead, I rethought my whole collecting philosophy, and, since that day, I've bought only what I enjoy, and I've had a lot more fun with the hobby.

"Collect what you enjoy," I said. "That's the key. Too many people lose sight of that or never understand it in the first place."

We reached the end of the aisle. The bourse was teeming with collectors avidly pursuing their individual goals.

"So, it's not whether you win or lose that's important," Paul said, "but how you enjoy the hobby."

"I think you've got it," I said. "And don't worry, one of these days, you'll get the gold."

And I'm sure he will.

Chapter 9

Nearly two decades ago, when my wife and I lived in our first house, one of our neighbors, on learning I was a stamp dealer, mentioned his aunt in California had a hoard of stamps. To hear Bob tell it, she had thousands, even hundreds of thousands of stamps. He never mentioned a value but hinted that, because of their sheer bulk, they were worth a considerable sum.

"Don't forget to tell your aunt you have a neighbor in the stamp business," I'd remind him as we stood sprinkling the dry spots on our lawns on warm summer evenings after supper. "I'd appreciate the opportunity to make an offer if she ever decides to sell."

"Don't worry," he'd say. "I've told her about you."

My wife, Sue, and I were young then. We had been married only a few years and had two small children, sons Steve and Mike. I was getting established in the stamp business, and we lived on the frugal side of comfortable, putting every extra cent into the business.

Then, one February evening, Bob called with the news that his aunt, Ruth Michaels, had decided to sell.

"Give her a call," he said. "She's expecting to hear from you."

I got on the phone right away. I learned that she lived alone in Indio, California. Her main social outlet was a correspondence she had carried on with a vast network of other collectors over the years. She collected mint stamps of the world and religiously ordered new issues from both dealers and foreign postal administrations. She bought multiples and actively traded with friends at home and abroad. She had accumulated thousand of stamps over the years. She was getting old, her eyesight was failing, and the time had come to sell. She wanted to know how soon I could come to see the stamps. It was a Tuesday, and I told her I could be there Friday. "Good," she said, "Come ahead."

After I'd hung up, I told Sue I was going to California to buy a collection. "Sounds like a good one. Plenty of stock. Just what I need."

"How much will it cost?"

"Don't know. Thousands, I'm sure."

Sue groaned silently. She'd grown used to me chasing after stamp deals with our savings, but she was never completely comfortable with the idea.

"Leave me with enough to pay the bills," she'd say, whenever I'd go.

"Don't worry," I'd say, but I knew she worried anyway.

"What if you don't buy the stamps? Trips aren't cheap."

"I'll close the deal," I said, confidently. In those days, I chased leads relentlessly, pressed to close every deal as if my life depended on it, and felt a great sense of defeat if one got away, which they did with regularity.

"You're talking about our life savings," she once said when I excitedly told her about a collection I had a chance to buy. It would take every cent we had. "How do you know you'll be able to get your money out of it?"

"I will, believe me."

She just shook her head as if I'd lost my mind and said, "Steve, I don't think this is a very good idea."

Finally, I said, "Okay, I'll spread the risk. I'll take in a partner."

A dealer friend put up fifty percent of the money, and we shared profits fifty-fifty. We bought the collection, got our money back in less than two weeks, and made twenty-five percent on the deal.

"See, everything turned out all right," I said, afterward. "I'd have made twice as much if I hadn't taken in a partner."

"Perhaps," she said, "Or maybe you were just lucky."

Now, more than twenty years later, we laugh about it.

I planned to drive south to Albuquerque, west to Flagstaff, south to Phoenix, then west to Indio. I would leave Wednesday morning, stay in Albuquerque the first night, reach Indio the second night, and meet with Ruth Michaels Friday morning.

The first day went according to plan. The following morning, I headed west, through Gallup, then detoured south on U.S. 666 to avoid snowy weather in the mountains near Flagstaff.

About halfway to Phoenix, the car suddenly shuddered violently. A terrible thumping racket came through the floorboards, as if someone was banging with a hammer. The car swerved. I fought to control the steering wheel, then the noise stopped as suddenly as it began. In my rearview mirror, I saw a large hunk of black rubber tumble out from behind the car. I'd run over a piece of retread thrown from the tire of a semi-trailer. The collision occurred during a moment's inattention, while I glanced at my map.

I pulled over to check for damage. Angry black swatches marked the places where the flailing retread had banged against the underside of the car. On its way under the car, it had whacked the universal joint, which appeared to be leaking fluid, although only slowly. I proceeded down the road, but after a few miles, the car didn't feel right, so I pulled over.

Great! I thought. *Stuck out in the middle of nowhere.*

Traffic was sparse. I didn't know how long it would be before a highway patrolman came along, so I tried flagging down passing motorists. No one paid any attention. I got a sinking feeling I wasn't going to make it to Indio that evening.

I was surprised when an 18-wheeler stopped.

"Got a problem?" the driver said.

"Yeah. Ran over a retread. Think it knocked something out under the car. I better have it towed."

"Hop in. There's a place down the road with a wrecker."

I swung myself up into the cab, listened to the airbrakes swoosh and the engine grunt as the driver eased it up through the gears.

Fifteen minutes later, we pulled into the gravel-covered drive of the Last Chance Cafe. The sign read: "Gas—Oil—Fine Food." A single row of gas pumps stood in front of the cafe, which was flanked by a two-bay garage on one side and several motel cabins on the other. Next to the garage was an array of screened cages on stilts, which presumably housed reptiles or small animals. The tow truck parked in front of the garage, its white paint gone flat in the Arizona sun, looked like it belonged in museum.

The semi ground to a halt. I stepped down from the cab, thanked the driver, and headed for the garage.

"I need a tow," I told the mechanic. "Ran over a retread."

"No problem," he said, wiping his hands on a red oil-rag, which he shoved into the back pocket of his coveralls. The name "Pop" was embroidered in a grimy white oval above his left pocket. "Whereabouts is your car?"

"Fifteen miles up the road," I said, pointing back the way I'd come.

As we walked toward the tow truck, he turned his head and spit tobacco juice, wiping, with the red rag, a stray droplet off the black stubble near the corner of his mouth. The tow truck started right away, which surprised me, and we drove off down the road at a leisurely pace. I was anxious to get the car checked and get back on the road, but Pop didn't share my sense of urgency. He took his own sweet time.

"There it is!" I said the moment my car came into view.

"We'll get her loaded in a jiffy," Pop said as he eased the truck onto the shoulder behind my car. He carefully hitched it to the tired old wrecker, which never exceeded forty miles an hour on its way back to the garage. He hoisted the car up on the lift and walked around underneath it, poking here and there, muttering.

Looking into the garage from outside was like looking into a small dark cave. A sign on the wall, almost lost among automotive girlie calendars and pinups, read "No customers in the work area." But Pop didn't object as I stood nearby watching him perform his inspection.

"Looks like you knocked out the seal . . . it's leaking, anyway. I'd have to pull it to know just how bad it is. That'll take fifteen or twenty minutes. Why don't you go on over to the cafe and have a cup of coffee? I'll let you know when I'm done."

I took a booth near the front window. An amiable, middle-aged waitress served me a 7-Up. While I waited, I checked my map. I'd planned to get to Indio at about eight that night, but, depending on how long it took to repair the car, it might be as late as midnight.

Half an hour later, the phone rang and from behind the counter, the waitress said, "Pop's done with your car."

"Thanks," I said, hurrying out. My bad luck had put me an hour and a half behind schedule.

"Seal's shot," Pop said. "You're gonna need a new one."

"Oh, great! How much will that cost?"

"Seal's about five bucks, plus twenty to install it."

"Okay," I said, relieved. "Go ahead. How long will it take?"

"About twenty minutes . . . after I get the part."

"And how long will that take?"

"Well, that's the problem. I'll have to call down to Phoenix for it. If they've got it in stock, it'll be on the bus first thing tomorrow. Bus gets in here around eleven, and I can have you out of here by eleven thirty. If they've got to get it from the warehouse, it might not get here until Monday."

"I have to be in Indio by tomorrow. Can't you just fix the seal?"

"Nope. It's bent. That's why it leaks. No way straighten it—it's shot."

"How far can I get on it?"

"Maybe a hundred miles, maybe a thousand, or might not last ten miles. Hard to say. But when it goes, your gonna make hamburger outta your rear end, and it'll cost a helluva lot more than twenty-five bucks to fix."

"Okay, go ahead and get the part from Phoenix."

While Pop checked on the part, I went back to the cafe and called Mrs. Michaels from a pay phone.

"I've had car trouble in Arizona," I said. "I won't be able to get there tomorrow like I planned. It may be Saturday or even as late as Tuesday."

"Oh, dear," Mrs. Michaels said. "Frank—he's a friend of mine—is driving me down to Los Angeles Monday. I made an appointment with a dealer there to look at the stamps. Frank goes to Los Angeles only two or three times a year, and Monday's one of those trips."

I got an icy feeling. Even if I'd arrived on schedule, Mrs. Michaels wouldn't have sold the collection to me, not with the Los Angeles trip lined up. My offer was Plan A. Los Angeles was Plan B. I also knew that if I showed up late, the collection would be history, sold to the dealer in Los Angeles. The only chance I had, and it seemed to be a long shot, was to get there before she went to Los Angeles Monday.

"You didn't mention that you were shopping for offers. I'm beginning to think I've made a trip for nothing."

"Well, I don't know that I'm shopping. I just thought it prudent to get several opinions."

"I wish you'd told me that before I invested my time and money in this trip."

"I'm sorry," she said. "It never occurred to me."

We talked for a few more minutes. She didn't think she wanted to change her plans to go to Los Angeles.

"I'll be here all weekend. Surely you can make it by Sunday?"

"That all depends on the part. It has to come from Phoenix. If it gets here tomorrow, I'll be there Saturday. If not, the earliest would be Tuesday."

I told here I'd get back to her when I learned more about the repair. Then, I hung up. I walked over to the garage to see how Pop was doing with the part.

"No luck so far," he said.

"Can't you get it from a regular parts store?"

"No, it's a dealer item."

"So when will we know?"

"Well, got one of my buddies checking around. He's gonna give a ring back."

"Can't you call other dealers while you're waiting?"

"Hey, it's long distance to Phoenix."

"I'll pay for the calls."

"I'd just be calling the same places my buddy's checking. We'll know in an hour or so. Why don't you go ahead and get a room. You're gonna be here tonight, anyway."

I walked out of the garage and glanced at the motel office. It looked dark.

"The office looks closed," I said, turning to Pop.

"Just tell Annie—the gal at the lunch counter—that you need a room. We don't get all that much traffic, so she don't keep the office open all the time," he said, smiling. His face, covered by stubble and grime, blended in with the gloom. Only his teeth contrasted with the dim interior of the garage.

I returned to the cafe thinking that Pop might not be trying as hard as he could to find the part. After all, how often did the Last Chance Motel have a shot at a three-day guest?

Annie pulled a guest register from under the lunch counter and signed me in.

"How long you staying?" she asked.

"Just tonight . . . I hope."

"Okay," she said. "That'll be fifteen bucks."

I reached for my wallet.

"I forgot to mention. We don't have room service, but the cafe's open until ten."

I walked back to the garage to retrieve my luggage and learned that Pop still hadn't heard from his buddy in Phoenix. My room, like the Last Chance Cafe, looked tired. The knotty pine decor looked out of date, rather than rustic. The bed was covered with a faded green spread that had been washed too many times. The bathtub sported legs, and the bathroom window was painted shut, the victim of too many successive coats of heavy white enamel. I began to resign myself to being stranded in Last Chance all weekend, losing the collection I'd driven hundreds of miles to buy, and ending up with nothing to show for the trip except auto-repair and motel bills.

Half an hour later, I went back to check on Pop. His feet were sticking out from under an El Camino.

"Heard from Phoenix yet?"

"Nope," he said, rolling himself out from under the car. "What time is it anyway?"

"Four-fifteen," I said, looking at my watch.

"Damn. He shoulda called by now."

"Maybe you should give him a call?"

"Yeah, well, it's long distance. It's no big deal for those guys at the dealership, but I'm a little guy."

"I'll pay for the call." I fought to keep my voice from rising. I felt that a deal worth thousands of dollars was slipping through my fingers over the cost of a fifty-cent long-distance call.

"Okay, okay," he said, walking over to the desk. He ran his finger across the dirty, doodle-covered desk pad until he found the number. Then, he dialed.

"Lemme talk to Phil," he said. Then, "Well, when will he be back?"

I wanted to scream. I was twisting ever-so-slowly in the wind in a place called Last Chance, Arizona, at the mercy of a man who seemed to be about as motivated as a thirteen-year-old dog on a hot summer afternoon.

"Tell him to call you right away," I interjected, "whether he's found the part or not. I've got to know what's going on!"

Pop scowled at me, then said into the receiver, "Listen, tell Phil to gimme a call the minute he gets back. I gotta talk to him." Then, he hung up.

"Keep your shirt on, mister. It ain't gonna do no good to holler at me. We'll find the part, and I'll fix your car just as quick as I can. In the meantime, the whole world ain't gonna come screeching to a halt just because you're in a big hurry."

"I've got to get to California this weekend," I said. "Monday's too late. The deal I'm working on will be long gone by then. I'm sorry if I raised my voice, but it seems like this parts problem just drags on and on."

"I'm doing the best I can. Why don't you go over to the cafe and have some coffee. Tell Annie it's on the house. Phil'll get back to me any minute now, and I'll let you know just as soon as he does. It ain't gonna do no good to get your blood pressure up."

I took Pop up on his offer. There wasn't anything else to do. I opted for an orange soda instead of coffee. Except for me, the cafe was deserted.

"Pop getting ya fixed up?" Annie asked, as she served the soda.

"I guess so. He's trying to locate a part in Phoenix."

We chatted. Annie was thin, in her late forties, wore a peach-colored uniform with white trim, kept a pencil tucked in her hair behind her ear, and gave the impression that life had passed her by like the traffic that zoomed by the Last Chance Cafe.

"What line of business you in—if you don't mind my asking?"

"Deal in stamps."

"For collectors?"

I nodded, sipping my soda.

"Lady next door to me used to collect stamps," she said, leaning on the counter behind her. "She even had a couple of those stamps with trains and ships upside down."

My ears perked up.

"One was on a postcard, least I think it was. She had lots of stamps, but that was her favorite."

"You saw it?" I visualized a 1-cent or 2-cent Pan American invert on a card or cover.

"Sure, lots of times."

"Does she still have the stamps?"

"Don't know. That was a long time ago. She talked about giving the whole collection to her son, *if* he ever got interested in stamps. But he never did—even after he grew up. He was too busy wheelin' and dealin' and chasing girls."

"So, she might still have the collection?"

"Could be. I don't know. Haven't seen her in years. Said if her son didn't get interested in stamps, she was going to sell the collection before she died. She was afraid he'd let it go for peanuts."

The bell on the front door jangled as a deputy sheriff walked in.

"Hi, Larry," she said walking over to serve him.

I thought about the inverts. The story sounded far-fetched, but I'd learned never to discount leads. Occasionally, opportunities struck like lightning. It seemed like a long shot, but maybe I could track down the lady with the inverts.

"Could you introduce me to your friend?" I asked, when Annie returned.

"That was years ago, when I lived in Phoenix. I don't know if she's still living, or even at the same address."

"I'm going through Phoenix," I said. "I'd like to get in touch with her, at least leave my name in case she's ever in the market to sell.

"Well, her name was Cromwell—Evelyn Cromwell. She might still be there. I haven't thought about her in years."

"Do you have her phone number?"

"I might, somewhere. I'd have to look for it."

"Would you? I'd sure appreciate it."

"Sure," she said, smiling. "I'll look for it tonight. You'll be in for breakfast tomorrow, won't you?"

"You bet."

About that time, Pop strolled into the cafe and told me Phil had found the part. "It'll be on the bus first thing tomorrow," he said.

I finished the soda and returned to my room. I decided not to call Mrs. Michaels until the part actually showed up and I knew for certain when I'd be in Indio. Instead, I called Sue.

"Bit of bad luck," I said. "Car broke down, but it looks like I'll be back on the road tomorrow."

"Where are you?"

"In Arizona, a place called the Last Chance Cafe . . . and Motel, Garage, Bus Stop, and Reptile Farm." I laughed.

"I knew something like this would happen," Sue said, sounding concerned.

"Don't worry, everything will be fine."

Suddenly, things were looking up. At least, I'd get to see Mrs. Michaels' collection, although I hadn't figured out how to solve the problem of her trip to Los Angeles. And I might just get a lead on some inverts.

Early the next morning, I looked out my front window and was surprised to see the cafe's dusty parking lot full of vehicles: two sheriff's cars, a telephone company truck, a beverage distributing company truck, and an assortment of cars and pickup trucks. I decided to wait until the crowd thinned before talking to Annie about her friend with the invert. I couldn't leave until after eleven, anyway, when the part from Phoenix was due to arrive.

By nine-thirty, the parking lot had emptied except for a lone highway patrol car, so I strolled across the gravel drive to the cafe.

"Have a nice night?" Annie asked cheerfully as I came through the front door.

"Just fine," I said.

Actually, I'd lain awake alternately worrying about how I'd put together the deal in Indio, and dreaming about what I'd do with the inverts I hoped to buy from Annie's friend.

I took a seat at the far end of the counter, eight stools away from the highway patrolman, and ordered pancakes.

"Were you able to find Mrs. Cromwell's phone number?" I asked, when Annie served the pancakes.

"I looked and looked," she said. "I know I've got it somewhere, but I just couldn't put my hands on it."

I was disappointed.

"I'll keep trying," she said.

"Thanks."

"Say," Annie said, "Don't be picking up any hitchhikers. Right, Roy?" She looked down the counter at the highway patrolman.

"Just asking for trouble if you do," the trooper said, nodding. "Best thing is just to keep on going."

"Hitchhiking's bad news. Isn't that what I've been telling you, honey?" Annie said, directing her remarks to a young woman seated in the booth behind me. The young woman appeared to be in her late teens or early twenties, wore a loose paisley shirt, blue jeans, sandals, and a red bandanna tied Indian-style around her head. Accents of blond ran through her long, straight brown hair, which came almost to her waist, and her eyes, the lightest shade of blue I'd ever seen, looked other-worldly.

"Just asking for trouble," Annie repeated. "Specially a pretty young gal like you."

"How long do you think it'll take to find Mrs. Cromwell's phone number?" I asked. "I'd really like to talk to her."

"I don't know. I'll just have to keep looking. It might be gone for all I know. It's been such a long time."

"Would you mind if I called in a few days? If you find it, maybe I could get together with her on my back from California."

"Sure," Annie said, smiling. Then, leaning down toward me, she said, "You know, I've been thinking—you're headed out to California, right?" I nodded. "Marianne over there is headed out to California, too. Maybe you could give her a ride?"

Oh, no, I thought. *No hitchhikers.* I started to shake my head.

"Says she's a singer, wants to get into the entertainment business. I just can't stand the thought of her hitchhiking, and she doesn't seem to know any better. I thought maybe you could give her a ride as far as you're going. You *are* headed toward L.A., aren't you?"

"Yes, but—"

"I'm sure she wouldn't be any trouble."

I turned and glanced at Marianne. She looked like a refugee from a protest march. She'd propped her guitar and duffel bag on the opposite seat of her booth.

"I don't think so . . ."

"Oh, come on," Annie said. Then before I could answer, she straightened up and called out to the young woman, "Marianne, come here a minute, honey." The young woman slid out of the booth and walked over to the stool next to me.

"This young fella's headed to Indio, and I thought he might be nice enough to give you a lift, at least that far."

"That would be nice," Marianne said, extending a slender, willow-branch of a hand. "I'm Marianne." She smiled.

I introduced myself and shook her hand, thinking her name ought to be something like Moon Flower. Annie grinned, and I knew I was trapped.

"I'll be leaving sometime after eleven, when my car's fixed. Meanwhile, I've got to pack and make some phone calls, so why don't I meet you here about eleven-fifteen?

"That's cool," Marianne said, "I'm not going anywhere."

What next? I thought, as I headed back to my room. I called Mrs. Michaels, explained that if the car were fixed on schedule, I'd be in Indio by that evening and could meet with her the next morning. I promised to give her a call to confirm it when I got into Indio. She said that would be fine and that she looked forward to getting together.

The new seal arrived on time the next morning. Pop fixed the car, I said goodbye to Annie, loaded Marianne's duffel bag into the back seat, and we set out for Indio.

Marianne didn't talk much at first. She quietly hummed tunes with her eyes closed, her head gently swaying from side to side with the rhythm. When I'd gone into the stamp business, I never dreamed I'd be driving across the middle of nowhere chasing a flaky lead, accompanied by a hippie on her way to Hollywood in search of fame and fortune.

"I'm going to stop for a burger," I said, after a while. "Would you like one?"

"No, thanks. Got some granola. I'm not into meat."

"You don't mind if do?" I asked, rhetorically.

"Not at all. Everyone's got their own trip. Live and let live."

She returned to humming the melody from *Both Sides Now.*

Later in the day, after we had passed Blythe and headed into the California desert, I said, "Annie told me you're a singer, that you're trying to get into show business."

She nodded.

"Kind of a long shot, isn't it?"

"Karma," she said, looking at me with her pale-as-early-morning-sky eyes. "It's karma."

"Karma?"

"There's a karmic tapestry for each of us. It's composed of the great universal fabric. We weave our own pattern on it," she said, in a tone as tenuous as her pale eyes. "It's kind of cosmic." She moved her arms in a sweeping circular motion.

"Cosmic consciousness," she said. "That's how I know where I'm going. You dig?" She looked at me, waiting for me to acknowledge that I understood.

"I'm afraid I don't know much about that," I said.

"A broad universal river carries us downstream through time. When you achieve cosmic consciousness, you come to understand that you can guide your fate, like a boat on that river. You begin to know where the river is taking you."

"It's a little beyond me," I said.

"It's not that hard," Marianne said. "You've got to meditate. That's the path to cosmic consciousness. You've got to screen out all the distractions, concentrate on a single point.

"Here, I'll show you," she said earnestly. "Sit straight, cross your legs, rest your hands and arms like so, take a deep breath, clear your head, and detach yourself from the external."

She kicked off her sandals, crossed her legs underneath her, rested her hands palms up in her lap, closed her eyes, and began chanting softly, "Oommm, oommm.

"It helps to have a *mantra,"* she said, opening her eyes. "I use 'oommm.' It helps you focus, screen out the irrelevant." She chanted "oommm" several more times.

"And by doing this you can see the future, see a career in show business?" I asked. It sounded hocus-pocus to me.

"You don't exactly see the future. You get in tune with the universe, with destiny. You get a feeling, it's like part of your being, a knowing of what you were meant to do. It's karma. You dig what I'm saying?"

"I guess so," I said, not really knowing what she meant, but trying to be agreeable.

"Anyway, think of your mind as a pool of water. It's all muddy from being stirred up by the daily hassles of life. So you meditate. You calm the pool, make it still, without ripples. Then the sediment settles, and the water becomes crystal clear. You relax, and, suddenly, everything is bathed in pure transcendental light. Universal truth reveals itself."

She looked at me with her light, transparent eyes. "It's hard to describe, but it's really a trip. You ought to try it sometime."

"And that's how you know you're going to make it in show business?"

"Yeah. I'd like to get into acting, too. I don't know exactly how everything will turn out, but L.A.'s where it's happening, so that's where I'll start. Once I get there, everything will unfold," she said with confidence.

We drove and the miles slipped by. Eventually, we arrived in Indio. I asked Marianne where she'd like to be dropped. "Anywhere's fine," she said, so I pulled over on the main street and let her out.

"Thanks for the ride. And remember, when you get hassled, meditate. It's good karma."

"I'll remember that," I said. "And good luck."

I checked into a motel, called Mrs. Michaels to confirm our meeting the next morning, and got directions to her home. As I lay in bed waiting for sleep, I wondered what I could say to convince her to sell to me rather than to the dealer in Los Angeles. I still didn't have an answer by the next morning when I arrived at her home.

She showed me into a bedroom converted into a stamp study, and I began going through the accumulation. Mrs. Michaels collected by country (Great Britain, France, San Marino, Russia, Czechoslovakia, among others) and by topic (flowers, medicine, scientists, ships, to name a few). She had dozens of albums and stockbooks, but the best part of the accumulation was a vast stock of duplicates, still in original glassines, some dating back as far back as 1950. They were roughly organized by country or topic, stored in small file cabinets, and tucked in boxes.

"There's no rhyme or reason to it," Mrs. Michaels said, as I poked here and there. "But I know where most everything is."

I worked steadily, carefully. I knew that the more time you spend evaluating a complex collection, the more precise your offer. When you rush, you tend to make conservative assumptions about value to protect yourself.

Thousands of colorful, common-looking, foreign sets peeked out as I riffled through handful after handful of glassines, but I noticed good sets, too. In the midst of a bunch of glassines cataloguing a few dollars, high-catalogue stamps, such as the Austrian bird airmails, popped up. Sometimes, the same set would appear in different places. The more I worked, the more I appreciated what a marvelous accumulation it was. I wanted to buy it in the worst way.

Mrs. Michaels was pleasant woman. She served me a sandwich for lunch, entertained me with anecdotes about her experiences corresponding with collector friends, and made me feel welcome. But when it came to the stamps, she was businesslike.

"I'm selling my home, liquidating the stamps, as well as some other assets. I no longer have confidence in my ability to look after myself alone here. I'm moving into a retirement center. It's expensive, so I've got to get the best price I can."

By late afternoon, I'd finished. My calculations totaled more than $15,000, which was more than I had at the time. The rest of my capital was tied up in inventory. I felt confident that I could borrow the extra money from my bank, but I wouldn't know for sure until I called them Monday. By then it would be too late.

"You've got a wonderful collection, Mrs. Michaels," I said. "I'd love to buy it, but I'd like to think about it overnight. I could come back tomorrow morning, if that's okay, and we could talk about it then?"

She thought for a moment, then said, "All right. Tomorrow's fine."

I called Sue that night.

"Did you buy the collection?" she asked.

"No, not yet. It may not work out. It's worth fifteen thousand. I've only got twenty-five hundred, plus the ten-thousand-dollar line of credit at the bank. I think the bank would give me the extra twenty-five hundred, but I won't know until Monday.

"And there's another problem. She has her mind set on taking the accumulation to Los Angeles Monday for another offer. I don't see how I'm going get around that."

"Well, you can't win 'em all. If it doesn't work, it doesn't work," Sue said, trying to sound upbeat.

"But it's such a gorgeous lot . . . and I've come so far."

"There'll be other collections."

"I know, but this one's right here, right now."

"Get some sleep and give it your best shot tomorrow. That's all you can do. Give me a call when you know how it turns out."

I slept fitfully, tossing between dreams of what I would do with Mrs. Michaels wonderful stock and despairing over the hopelessness of the situation. The next morning I drove to her home feeling that no matter what I said, I'd lose the deal.

"Come in, Mr. Datz," Mrs. Michaels said, showing me into the dining room. "Have a seat. I'll get some tea, and we can talk."

I thought about the albums and boxes and about the difficulties I'd had getting this far. I tried to compose my thoughts. I just had to buy the collection.

I closed my eyes and took a deep breath. *Let the sediment settle. Let the water clear.* That's what Marianne had said. *Just relax, and let the ripples fade. You'll see everything in pure transcendental light.* I took another deep breath and relaxed. Suddenly, I realized I'd been concentrating on the collection and dithering about the Los Angeles dealer too much. I needed to change my focus. I needed to think about Mrs. Michaels. After a few moments, everything fell into place, and I knew what I must do.

"Have you thought it over, Mr. Datz?" Mrs. Michaels said, setting the tea on the table in front of me, bringing me out of my contemplation.

"Yes, I have," I said, ignoring the tea, looking directly at her. "You have a wonderful collection. It's just what I need at this stage in my career. I know you're planning to take it to Los Angeles tomorrow, but I think you'd get a better price from me."

"I don't know. The store in Los Angeles is large, and they've been in business a long time."

"That's just the point. To a large dealer, it's just another collection. He'll look at it, make an offer, and if you walk out, no problem, he can live without it. He won't stretch to buy it. I will.

"I'm just getting started and could really use the stock. I went through it very carefully so I could make you the best possible offer. The man in L.A. won't spend as much time on it as I did. He'll miss things and bid on instinct. But I know what's there. I've included every last stamp in my offer."

"I'm sure you have, Mr. Datz, but you're quite young. The dealer in Los Angeles has had much more experience." I could see skepticism in her eyes.

"Just because I'm young doesn't mean I don't know stamps. I've been collecting since I was twelve years old. I went into business when I got out of college. All in all, I've got quite a few years' experience. If you stop and think about it, my youth works to your benefit. I'm highly motivated to buy your collection. I'm willing to make a generous offer."

"How much?" she asked.

"Fifteen thousand dollars."

She remained thoughtfully silent for a moment, then said, "I really ought to get a second offer."

"That would be prudent, but this trip has cost more than I anticipated. I can't afford to wait around until Tuesday. If the L.A. offer is lower, you'll be out of luck."

She remained silent.

"Did you have a figure in mind?" I asked.

She looked up at me. "Yes, I'd hoped to get at least ten thousand out of it."

"Well, I've offered you half again as much. I don't think you'll find anyone who'll give you more."

She considered.

"You're talking cash, of course?"

"I can give you twelve thousand, five hundred now, and the balance no later than two weeks."

Her brow wrinkled.

"Your nephew, Bob, can vouch for me. We've been neighbors for three years. Or if you like, you can keep part of the stamps until I send the balance. What do you say, Mrs. Michaels? Can we do business?"

"Well, you're a persistent young fellow, I'll give you that," she said. After a moment's silence she said, "All right, I'll take your offer."

I wanted to jump for joy. I wrote a check for $12,500 and an IOU for the balance.

"Go ahead and take all the stamps," she said. "I'm sure I can trust you for the balance."

"Thank you," I said. Then, I condensed the glassines into cardboard boxes, and tried to make everything else as compact as possible to fit in my car.

"Thanks again," I said after I'd loaded the accumulation into my car and was ready to leave. "Your collection will be a big help to me."

"I had a feeling it would," she said. "That's why I sold it to you—that, and the price."

I was on the road before noon. I decided to drive as far as the Last Chance Cafe, stay overnight, and talk to Annie about her friend's telephone number.

"Looks like you bought the collection," Annie said, when I walked into the cafe.

"Yup. And now I'm hoping you'll have good news for me. Any luck with Mrs. Cromwell's phone number?"

"Darndest thing," Annie said, pausing from wiping the counter. I've looked everywhere, but I just can't seem to find it. I know it'll turn up, and when it does, I'll call you."

Then, she said, "Ride with Marianne go okay?"

"Yeah," I said, shaking my head. "She's a little far-out. And I wasn't too happy about the way you Shanghaied me into taking her. But, it worked out."

Annie laughed.

"Hated to see her hitchhike. Besides, I got a soft spot for kids with dreams. If you ain't got dreams, you ain't got nothin'," she said, as she resumed wiping the counter.

Chapter 10

Over the years, I've known many people who've wanted to get into the stamp business. I can't begin to count them. Most have long since dropped out, and I've concluded the reason is that they know a lot about stamps, but little about business. They'd stand a better chance if it was the other way around.

Clark Sawyer wanted to be a stamp dealer in the worst way. He was a fresh-faced, well-groomed, button-down-collar kind of kid. He arranged with a coin dealer to give him some space to set up his stamp business. Clark chose one of the most upscale coin dealers—who I'll call American National Coin Company—in the city. Clark set up shop behind a display counter in a corner of the elegant store. American National Coin reminded me of Tiffany's: staff in tailored three-piece suits, deep-pile carpeting that deadened all sound, polished glass counter tops, stunning gold and silver coins arrayed on royal blue velvet, upholstered chairs at counters.

Clark was in his early twenties, cheerful, reasonably good looking, and well dressed. What he lacked in knowledge he made up for in eagerness to learn. He was thrilled to be in American National Coin, and he fit well—almost. Clark's only problem was that the quality of his inventory was not on par with the quality of American National's coins.

Being a neophyte to stamp dealing, Clark—like so many others new to the business—set up shop using his collection as stock. Unfortunately, Clark lacked the kind of stamps American National's discriminating customers expected to see—high-profile, high-ticket items. And I suspect that American National wasn't terribly thrilled about having their counters crowded with collectors rummaging through Clark's 3-cents-a-stamp boxes. Clark told me that his arrangement with American National included paying them a percentage of the profits from stamp sales. The monthly percentage couldn't have been much, probably a fraction of what American National expected.

After a few months, Clark vacated American National and moved in with another coin dealer, Norbert Dean McCall. McCall hated the name Norbert, preferring to be called Deano. Deano's operation was poles apart from American National's. He operated out of a storefront in a shopette a decade past its prime. A garish, oversized, bright yellow sign in the shape of a twenty-dollar gold piece perched above his front door. The name *Deano's Coins* wrapped around the top of the sign. The store was furnished with outmoded display cases filled with a patchwork of red, black, and blue coin trays. Tired-looking supplies hung from wire holders on once-white, perforated-masonite walls. The window display, judging from the layer of dust, hadn't been changed in years.

Deano loved wildly colored Hawaiian shirts and gold neck chains. He always had the short half of a cigar clenched between his teeth. Deano knew only one style—high-pressure. He seemed born and bred to it, like a pit bull. Had Deano not been a coin dealer, he would have been at home in the used car business.

Deano played the precious metals futures markets. "Hey, I'm gonna be a millionaire one of these days," he would say good naturedly in the kind of tone that left you unsure whether or not he was joking. He tirelessly extolled the virtues of precious metals to anyone within earshot. "Silver and gold are going through the roof, and when they do, those who were smart enough to get in early are going to make money in spades!" To the uninitiated, Deano sounded like an expert, but those who knew him took everything he said with a grain of salt.

Deano was never at a loss for words. No matter what the state of the market, he urged buyers and sellers to do business that day.

When the market was weak, he would say, "The market's down, down, down—perfect time to get in at the bottom. Upside's unlimited!" When the market was high, he would say, "Market's

hot, hot, hot—if you don't get in now, you'll only pay more later."
According to Deano any day was a good day to buy—or sell.

I once mentioned to Deano that his advice sounded a little
phony. He smiled and said, "Hey, they've already made up their
minds when they walk in the door. They just want someone to pat
'em on the back and tell 'em everything's going to be okay."

Deano won $10,000 the very first week the Colorado lottery
operated. He didn't think it unusual or himself lucky; he had a
system. He bought 500 lottery tickets a week. "You're bound to
get a winner if you buy enough tickets," he was fond of saying, as
if he had some secret monopoly on intelligence or intuition. After
that first week, however, Deano never had another big winner.

Initially, Clark seemed happy at Deano's. At least, his stock
was more on par with Deano's than it had been with American
National's. And Deano didn't mind Clark's nickel-and-dime-box
trade.

"How's business?" I asked one day about three months after
Clark had set up shop at Deano's.

"It's okay," Clark said, not sounding like he meant it. Then, "I
think I need more stock. The markup's great on all this cheap stuff,
but no matter how much of it I sell, it doesn't add up to any real
money."

Clark had learned what many new to the business learn. You
can't take cheap stamps—the dollar-a-thousand variety—and even
with astronomical markups, still make any real money. Even with
customers doing all the labor, the average sale is hardly worth the
effort. It just doesn't go far toward paying the high cost of retail
overhead.

"I jumped into this business without much thought about how
I'd go about it other than just put my own stamps up for sale and
buy what I needed." He had done the same thing many newcomers
to the business do; he'd jumped into the water without knowing
how to swim.

"How's it working out with Deano?" I asked.

"Okay, I guess," Clark said, glancing back at Deano's office.
"At least he keeps me entertained. He's always got a 'big' deal
cooking. Always a million bucks just around the corner." Clark
shrugged, palms upturned. "That's just Deano."

I smiled. I knew what he meant. What Deano lacked in substance, he made up in energy. He buzzed around the shop in his Hawaiian shirts like a frenetic bumblebee wearing butterfly's wings.

I sold Clark stamps and allowed him a return privilege, so he could get his feet wet without too much risk. I gave him advice and tried to help him get started. Clark had inherited $20,000 from his father, but he seemed cautious about spending too much of it on stock at once. Clark usually visited me about once a week to select new stock, and, occasionally, I would stop by and visit him.

One morning, while Clark and I were chatting, two men built like pro-football linebackers walked in and strode purposefully back toward Deano's office. They had the no-nonsense look of bouncers from a two-bit bar. They opened Deano's office door without knocking, went in, and slammed it shut behind them.

"Uh-oh," Clark said ominously, "you might not want to stick around."

"Oh?" I said. "Who are those guys?"

"Deano bounced on check Johnny Angel."

"You've got to be kidding! Only a fool would do that."

"Yeah, well, Deano lost a couple grand playing poker over at Johnny's last weekend—"

"Deano plays poker with Johnny Angel? He's got to be nuts!" I interrupted. Johnny Angel was the head of the local mob. Johnny and his compatriots had been in and out of the headlines, and in and out of prison over the years for loan sharking, extortion, gambling, and a host of other illegal enterprises. The nickname "Angel" was an antonymic appellation, like "Tiny" for a grossly overweight man. I knew just how nasty Johnny Angel could be. A friend of mine in the restaurant business had been approached by Johnny Angel's linen service. He refused to switch to Angel's service, so one night not long after, two of Angel's men caught him behind his restaurant and beat him viciously with bricks. He spent several days in the hospital. When he got out, he switched to Angel's linen service. Johnny Angel was not a man to fool around with.

"Those guys must be here to collect," Clark said.

"Doesn't Deano have better sense?" I said. "Didn't he know he would lose? Angel doesn't play poker for fun. Everyone knows he only plays poker with marks."

Clark shrugged. "Deano thought he could beat him—that's Deano for you. He's gotta live life in the fast lane, close to the edge."

"Losing's bad enough, but bouncing a check on Angel . . ." I shook my head. "He'd better pay up if he knows what's good for him."

"Well, that's the problem—Deano doesn't have the two grand. He's already asked me to lend him the money. That's how I know what happened. I was dumb enough to lend him four thousand last month, and I haven't gotten it back yet. He said he needed it to buy a collection at a show he was going to in Las Vegas. Said he could turn the collection fast and give me five grand back in less than a week. Well, that was three weeks ago, and he's only paid me five hundred. I realize now he blew the money gambling. Anyway, he's been on the phone all morning, trying to raise cash."

Clark ought to know better, too, I thought.

"Well, guess I better get going," I said. It was time to leave. I didn't want to be around when whatever happened to Deano happened.

Just then, the door opened, and the two grim-faced heavies strode out and headed for the front door. They walked right past Clark and me as if we didn't exist. As the front door swung shut behind them, a shaken, deathly pale Deano appeared in the doorway of his office. "Clark, can I see you for a minute?" he said in an uncharacteristically quiet voice.

"Sure," Clark said. "Are you okay?"

"Yeah, for the time being."

Clark disappeared into Deano's office. He was back a couple of minutes later.

"Angel wants three grand instead of the two Deano lost. The extra grand is a penalty for bouncing the check. The money's due Friday." It was Wednesday. Deano had two days to come up with the money.

"And if he doesn't?"

"They said they'd fix his knees so they'd bend both ways."

I didn't doubt they meant what they had said.

Later, Clark told me that that incident had crystallized his decision to look for new space. Deano wholesaled some coins—coins that, according to Clark, had been consigned to him—to raise the money to pay off Angel. He even managed to give Clark another $500. But Clark had had enough of the way Deano did business, and worried about his getting into more trouble with the likes of Johnny Angel. Clark didn't want to be in the fallout zone. He decided it was time to stop sharing space with coin dealers and get a shop of his own. So, he bought Nelson Wolfe's shop—The White Peak Stamp Company.

Wolfe had an unusual business specialty. He set up stamp shops, then sold them to newcomers at inflated prices. And he had it down to an art. He would rent a storefront, furnish it with attractive but inexpensive counters and chairs, decorate the walls with stamp-related memorabilia—enlargements of stamps, maps, etc.—and make the place warm and cozy. He'd stock the shelves with an appealing array of albums, supplements, mounts, and supplies worth perhaps $1,500. He'd fill the counters with bulging Tarifold displays crammed with shiny new stocksheets full of colorful topical sets and souvenir sheets, mostly from Eastern Europe or Persian Gulf states, the kind known as "Sand Dunes." Shelves behind the counter were lined with dozens of small, black three-ring counter books containing additional stock identified by country or topic. I once looked through Wolfe's counter books, but found nothing priced at more than a couple of bucks, and all of it available from wholesalers by the hundred or thousand. The whole operation couldn't have cost more than $7,500 to set up, probably a lot less.

Soothing, barely audible music played in the background. Wolfe, ever-smiling, tended customers with the quiet self-assurance of a knowledgeable, successful man. Middle-aged and just beginning to show a paunch, he greeted everyone who came through his front door as if they were long-lost friends. People liked Wolfe, and they felt at home in The White Peak Stamp Company.

Wolfe served serious collectors from a stock of better stamps he kept locked in a beige metal storage cabinet that stood unobtrusively in the rear of the store.

"Let me get you something from my private stock," he would say in a tone that made people feel like they were being treated to stamps especially reserved for preferred customers.

Clark regarded White Peak Stamp Company as the ideal model for the kind of store he would like to have. So, I suppose it was only natural that when Clark moved out of Deano's—in justifiable fear of life and limb—he wound up at Nelson Wolfe's. Wolfe took Clark under his wing, gave him a job of sorts—Clark had to work for free in exchange for Wolfe teaching him the business.

Clark must have been impressed by what he saw. About six weeks after he began at Wolfe's, he bought White Peak Stamp Company. I visited him shortly thereafter and learned that Clark had paid $25,000 for the business: $15,000 down and payments of $500 a month for two years on the balance.

"Sounds like a good deal," I told Clark. "Wolfe had some pretty good stuff in those stockbooks in the locker."

"Oh, the deal didn't include his personal stock," Clark said. "But I got everything else—Tarifold flippers, backup stock, counter books, supplies, furniture, fixtures, and goodwill. I'm tired of fooling around. Buying a going business was worth the extra cost."

I groaned silently. I didn't want to burst Clark's bubble by telling him that all he got for his money was about $7,500 worth of furniture, fixtures, questionable stock, and "goodwill."

Wolfe had done the same thing at least twice before that I was aware of. Amy Proctor had bought Cascade Mountain Stamps from Wolfe two years before. She had retired from teaching and looked forward to a pleasant, profitable second career in the stamp business. Like Clark, she had been a part-time helper in the store Wolfe eventually sold her. A few months after buying the store, she realized it wasn't going to make it. It didn't generate enough income to support itself, let alone service the debt owed Wolfe. On the surface, the operation looked great. The detail Wolfe had neglected to mention when he showed her his income state-ment—which was in the black—was that the greatest percentage of profit was derived from sales of stamps from his so-called private stock. Without those sales, not only did she not make a profit, but it took most of her monthly pension to meet overhead and service the debt she owed Wolfe. After less than a year in business, she closed the store and moved away. I never learned whether she paid Wolfe off or not. In any case, Wolfe had clearly taken advantage of her.

Wolfe sold his next store to Stuart Cremona. Cremona was thinking about leaving his profession, accounting, to take up stamps. After a few months in the shell company Wolfe sold him, he quickly abandoned the idea of a career in stamps. Fortunately, he hadn't burned his bridges before embarking on his ill-fated new career.

Wolfe set up his operations with the care and patience of a spider weaving a web, and he was as merciless. When a victim stumbled into his snare, he drained them dry without a moment's hesitation.

I never cared for Wolfe. I knew his game, and I didn't like it. Technically, he hadn't done anything illegal. He was careful to commit every detail of his stamp store sales to contracts drawn up by his attorney. He covered his bases well. Still, there was the matter of character.

And sometimes that is revealed in the smallest ways. Wolfe moved to another city shortly after selling White Peak Stamps to Clark. On his final weekend in town, Wolfe attended a stamp show at which I served as bourse chairman. I had rented a specific number of white tablecloths to cover the bourse tables. When the show was over, I set about retrieving the tablecloths so I could return them to the rental company. I retrieved all but the two that had been on Wolfe's table and backup table. He'd taken them with him, a fitting signature for his final appearance in Denver.

Clark learned a painful lesson. White Peaks Stamp Company lasted less than a year. Dispirited, his inheritance exhausted, Clark left the stamp trade more than a decade ago, and has not been heard from since.

Chapter 11

Although not everyone who enters the stamp business makes it, some do.

"That gentleman has a stamp for sale," an excited Charlie Byers informed me one Saturday afternoon at APEX in Aurora, Colorado. "Says he's got a C3a."

Scott No. C3a is the famous inverted Jenny airmail stamp. Charlie, a sharp young fellow in his mid-twenties, worked for me part-time. He wanted to learn the stamp business and was especially eager to gain experience in the art of buying.

I looked over at the waiting seller, who was standing at the far end of my two-table booth. Then I said to Charlie, "I'm tied up at the moment. You take care of him."

"I'm not qualified to handle a deal like that!" Charlie gasped.

"You said you wanted to learn how to buy," I replied. "You've got to get your feet wet sometime. No time like the present. Just don't overpay."

Charlie looked at me, mouth agape.

"Go ahead," I said. "You'll do fine."

Charlie swallowed hard and stepped back over to the man. "Do you have the stamp with you?" he asked.

"No," the man said. Then, "Actually, I have two inverted Jennies. I could bring them by tomorrow afternoon for you to look at, if you're interested. They've been in the family for years. I also have some other good stamps."

"That would be fine," Charlie said,

"About two o'clock?" the man asked.

"We'll be here."

"Okay," the mystery man said. "See you around two." They shook hands, and he walked off.

"He'll be back at two tomorrow," Charlie told me.

"Great," I said, "You handle the deal."

"Get serious!"

"I am. You wanted to learn how to buy, so I just tossed you into the pool. Now you've got to sink or swim."

Charlie looked nervous and expectant, as if waiting for me to let him off the hook.

"You'll do just fine," I said. "Don't worry about it."

The next morning, Charlie showed up in his best suit. As we ate breakfast, he dropped a big glob of jelly onto his tie. He swabbed the spot furiously with a napkin dipped in water, but the damage was done.

"Oh, great!" he said. "Now I look like a slob. What's the guy with the inverts going to think?"

"Don't worry about it. Take off the tie. It'll be okay."

"But I want to look professional."

"The man will be interested in how much you offer, not whether you're wearing a tie or not."

About half the dealers at shows don't wear ties. In fact, there's a running joke about how to tell whether a dealer is from east or west of the Mississippi. Eastern dealers wear ties, western dealers don't.

"But this is a big deal," Charlie said.

"Big deals are no different than small deals. Don't be nervous about the size of the deal. Just pretend it's an ordinary deal."

Charlie looked puzzled.

"If you start thinking about the size of the deal, you lose track of the fundamentals, which are the condition of the stamp, the amount you expect to re-sell it for, the amount of profit you'd like to make, how long you'll have to keep it, and whether you can buy the same item for less elsewhere. They're the same things I've told you before."

"Yeah, but there wasn't an inverted Jenny at stake."

"Nevertheless, the same business discipline applies. The seller has goals, too. If a mutually satisfactory middle ground exists, you'll do business. If not, you won't. You can't worry about it. Remember, there's always another deal, and there are always more stamps than you have money to buy. So don't lose your cool. If it doesn't work out, go on to the next deal."

I felt like a coach telling his quarterback to treat the championship final like any other game.

"Okay," Charlie said, dubiously.

"You can have my tie, if it'll make you feel any better."

"Naw, I'll wing it," he said, smiling, sounding more confident. "But how much should I pay?"

"Depends on the quality of the stamp."

"I know, but how will I know how much to pay?"

"I've given you some guidelines. Look at the stamp, and you'll know when the time comes. Just don't offer more than you would if it were your own money. Assume that if I don't like the price you paid, I'll ask you to buy it from me at that price."

Charlie gulped.

"And remember, I'm behind you one-hundred percent."

"You make it sound so easy."

"It is. Just don't get excited and lose your cool."

"What if I blow it? What if he walks because I screw up?"

"He won't."

We finished breakfast and headed for our booth. The morning went by quickly, and as two o'clock approached, Charlie nervously adjusted his suit, ran a comb through his hair every few minutes, and frequently checked his watch.

At five minutes to two, he said, "Look, this is crazy. You'd better handle the deal."

"You said you wanted to learn how to buy. You'll never get a better chance."

He didn't look impressed.

At ten minutes after two, he said, "Where is that guy, anyway?"

"Relax, it's Sunday afternoon. He'll get here when he gets here."

Charlie sighed a long, nervous sigh. More minutes passed. He paced the booth, checked his watch, and craned his neck to see if he could spot the man somewhere on the show floor.

At three o'clock, he said, "I wonder what happened?"

"He's not going to show," I said.

"He's not? How do you know?"

"That same guy came around last year and asked if I'd like to see not one, but two Jennies. Said he'd be back Sunday afternoon with the stamps, but never showed up."

"You mean you put me through this for nothing!" Charlie exclaimed.

I smiled.

"Of all the lousy tricks . . ."

"Consider it an initiation."

"I didn't get much sleep last night, I was so worried about this deal," Charlie said.

"But you were ready to give it a try. You had confidence."

"I was scared as hell."

"Don't sell yourself short. You were ready to go, and that's what buying is all about."

"You know what I think?"

I shook my head.

"I think you owe me dinner."

I chuckled and nodded.

"At the best steakhouse in town."

"You drive a hard bargain," I said. Charlie grinned, pleased with the compliment.

Charlie proved to be a capable buyer. He numbered among the few I've met with a natural talent for the stamp business, and I was never disappointed with any purchase he made during the time he worked for me.

Chapter 12

Buying trips offer, for me at least, a welcome change of pace from the hectic tempo of stamp shows. My fondness for driving through vast open spaces made it easy for me to agree to drive from Denver to Douglas, Wyoming, to buy Tom Shelby's stamp collection. According to Shelby, he had formed a solid intermediate Japanese collection. He also had $20,000 face value in Libyan stamps. The Japanese stamps interested me. The Libyan stamps . . . well, $20,000 worth sounds like a lot unless you know about Libyan stamps.

What a perfect day for a drive, I thought as I headed north on Interstate 25 past the neatly laid out farms, into the enormous sea of golden prairie. Delicate, gauzy cirrus clouds streaked the clear November sky. To the west, the Rockies appeared as gray-violet bluffs. To the east, the Pawnee National Grassland stretched to the horizon. More than 100 miles beyond it, near the Nebraska border, lay Julesburg, once a Pony Express station.

As I cruised along, it struck me that the landscape looked as empty as it must have more than a century before, when the Pony Express operated. Looking out my windshield, it was easy to imagine a lone rider traversing the featureless brown horizon at full gallop . . . .

The imaginary rider is not alone. A war party of Cheyenne or Sioux races to intercept him. They whoop and holler, urging their ponies on in frenzied pursuit. The young rider spurs his horse and, head low, races for his life. He prays his horse is faster, prays his lead will hold, prays for pony soldiers, but in his heart knows he is alone. His life depends on the speed of his horse, nothing else.

It's easy to visualize the scene, because, except for the interlude of 125 years and the ribbon of highway that divides the landscape ahead of me, the prairie hasn't changed. It's as if the golden sea is becalmed in time. Suddenly, I know the rider has a swift horse and, despite the Indians' efforts, wins the race and lives to tell his grandchildren about it. Will the recipients of the letters he carries appreciate that he risked his life to deliver them? Will any of the covers survive to be treasured by collectors? I like to think so.

Another thought intrudes.

"Desolate," Gary Casey had said, looking out across the same empty landscape. "Utterly desolate."

"Yeah," I had agreed, not wanting to contradict him. At the same time, I had thought *open, unspoiled, free.*

Gary and I had been driving to Cheyenne. Gary wanted to call on the large Unicover operation there to see if any business opportunities existed. The year was 1982 or 1983.

Gary, a native New Yorker completely at home in the bustling corridors of Manhattan, found the wide open spaces of Wyoming unsettling.

"What do you do if your car breaks down out here?" he asked.

"Sooner or later, someone will stop to see if you need help. People are neighborly in this part of the world."

Gary looked skeptical. I suspected his New York City street smarts didn't allow him to entirely believe me, a thought that amused me. I remembered my first trip from Kennedy Airport to midtown Manhattan. I'd never seen gutted automobile hulks on a freeway or graffiti-covered overpasses before.

On the way back from Cheyenne that day, Gary had said, "I'm sorry, I just can't get used to all this open space. It bothers me somehow, like claustrophobia in reverse."

I chuckled. I couldn't imagine anyone being made uncomfortable by open space. Manhattan gave me a vague sense of apprehensiveness. A man raised in America's empty quarter finds it difficult to get used to the city's concrete canyons even after dozens of visits. Impressions linger: intersections crowded with cars, none willing to give an inch; traffic cops tweeting their whistles, waving their arms, shaking their fingers at errant drivers, all in a hopeless attempt to orchestrate the chaos; taxis requiring dividers to protect drivers from fares; guards at shop doors; ubiquitous street vendors hawking everything from wind-up toys to imitation brand-name watches; corner three-card Monte games; and zombie-like crowds fearful of eye contact. And the subways . . . one hears too many stories about them, imagines them to be inhabited by morlocks, the horrific subterranean denizens of H.G. Wells's futuristic novel, *The Time Machine*.

But there is also the memorable New York City. The center of finance, art, culture, and stamps. The New York that boasts the world's finest restaurants, most wonderful museums and shows, and most fabulous stores. That is the New York City I enjoy, the city I look forward to visiting.

Those impressions, like the wispy cirrus clouds high in the morning sky, crossed my mind as I headed north to keep my appointment with Tom Shelby. I hoped I wasn't on a wild goose chase. Shelby had given the right answers on the phone. His collection sounded promising.

The drive to Douglas took nearly four hours. There was little traffic and lots of time to think that November morning. I reviewed what I would look for, rehearsed what I would say, hoped Shelby would be reasonable, and that I could close a deal. I wondered if he knew about Libyan stamps. I wondered if the drive would be worth it.

The highway seemed to stretch forever, rising and falling in gentle swells. As far as I could see, there was nothing but the land and sky. A mile ahead, a cream-colored Buick cruised at a steady 80 miles an hour. I kept pace behind it. The Buick's driver seemed unconcerned about speed traps. He knew, as I did, that there is so little traffic the highway patrol often doesn't bother to set up speed traps.

Will the trip be worth it? That's always the question, and you never know. Still, you've got to chase deals. If you wait for them to fall into your lap, they never do—and you end up just waiting and waiting. *It's probably different in the big city,* I thought. *There are plenty of deals to be done. But out here, there aren't as many people, not as many deals. You've got to go after them.*

I sped north past towns with names like Chugwater and Wheatland. Finally, Douglas came into view. On the way to Shelby's home, I passed a patchwork of dwellings, the kind that no one in this part of the world gives a second thought to: large homes next to small homes, mobile homes next to permanent structures. Pickups, horse trailers, motorcycles, snowmobiles sat wherever they were last parked. Some yards had lawns, others were dirt. But they're all in harmony if you understand that in rural western communities individualism is more highly prized than outward appearance. Tom Shelby's directions took me straight to his home, a small, robin's-egg-blue, frame structure with a waist-high chain link fence around the front yard.

Shelby greeted me at the door. "Come on in," he said, gripping my hand vigorously. He looked like a cowboy fresh from the rodeo circuit: slim, a youthful yet weathered face, plaid shirt with mother-of-pearl pocket snaps, and levis held up by a wide leather belt with an oversized bison buckle.

The interior of his home looked as disorganized as the appearance of the town. The utilitarian furnishings looked like they had been picked up at the local discount furniture store. A pair of crossed samurai blades and an oriental wall-hanging decorated one living room wall. A gun rack on another held a pump shotgun, a bolt action rifle, and a Winchester Model 30 lever-action carbine, the legendary weapon of the frontier.

"Have a chair," he said, motioning toward the kitchen table. "Would you like some coffee . . . or maybe a beer?"

"No, thanks," I replied, "perhaps a glass of water later."

"I was stationed in Japan," he said, seating himself at the kitchen table. "That's how I got interested in Japanese stamps." He pushed a bulging specialty album toward me. "Liked the artwork. Kinda simple and pretty . . . not all garbaged up."

I understood what he meant.

"I've got some better items—national parks, souvenir sheets, and that airmail set, the one with the zeros."

I opened the album and paged through it. The first few pages were empty, the next few sparse, then the tempo picked up. Beginning with the national parks set of 1936, the majority of spaces contained mint stamps.

"Picked up most of the stamps overseas," he said, as I turned the pages. While I looked at the album, he sipped black coffee and smoked a Winston, lifting his chin occasionally to exhale toward the ceiling.

The abundance of postwar issues pleased me. He had the "Moon and Geese" sheet and a comprehensive showing of key definitives, including 500-yen issues. Shelby had hinged most of his stamps except the souvenir sheets, which were mounted in plastic. The collection petered out around 1978.

"Kinda lost interest after I got back to the States," he said as I reached the back of the album. Then, "Now for the good stuff." He pushed a large manila envelope across the formica table top. He rose to pour himself another cup of coffee while I extracted a thick mass of Libyan stamps: sheets, souvenir sheets, imperfs, etc. Ghadafi's somber face, his expression appearing uncomfortable, peered out over desert dunes. I groaned silently.

"Got those in Libya," Shelby said. "Worked for Shell for a while, did some wheeling and dealing on the side. You can't take cash out of the country, so they paid me in stamps—twenty thousand dollars' worth face value. And there's all kinds of stuff you can't get over the counter—imperfs, odd colors, you name it."

Shelby beamed.

Unfortunately, Shelby's Libyan holding wasn't the first I had come across. Judging from the number of inquiries I'd had during the preceding months, it seemed clear that Libyans had paid many luckless, foreign dealmakers in stamps. One caller even claimed to have $50,000 worth at face value.

"Well, there's not much of a market for Libyan stamps right now," I said, hoping to let him down gently. I wanted to buy the Japanese collection but worried that the Libyan stamps, which were more or less worthless, would be a deal blocker. "Not too much demand for stamps with Ghadafi's portrait at the moment. And Libyan currency isn't convertible, so face value is hypothetical. I hate to say it, but you probably have a better chance of cashing in Confederate war bonds that getting anything out of your Libyan stamps."

Shelby's face fell.

"Don't feel bad. You're not the only one the Libyans paid in stamps. It happened to quite a few people."

"No wonder it was so easy to do the deal," Shelby said. "I figured I'd make a killing on all these imperfs, all this odd stuff they told me you can't get across the counter. Man, I fell for it hook, line, and sinker!" He exhaled a sigh of disgust.

"I'm still interested in the Japanese collection," I said. "There's some value there."

"Maybe I ought to keep the whole mess," Shelby said, seemingly lost in thought, his hand on his chin. His hand was streaked with minute black lines, as if crude oil had filled in the creases of the skin and remained despite repeated scrubbings. Then, he said, "I guess the stamps aren't doing me much good right now. I might as well sell 'em."

"How much do you want for the collection?" I asked.

Shelby looked at me for a moment, weighed his answer.

"I figured the whole mess ought to be worth somewhere in the neighborhood of twenty-five thousand."

I'd been afraid of that.

"Unfortunately, I can't use the Libyan stamps . . . at any price. I'd be willing to give you twenty-four hundred for the Japan."

"Twenty-four hundred? Boy, what a letdown. It doesn't seem like much."

"Most of the stamps are hinged."

"The souvenir sheets aren't."

"True, but they're only a small portion of the value." I extracted several retail advertisements for Japanese stamps from my attaché case. I put them on the table in front of him. "I'm offering fifty to sixty percent of retail for your stamps."

Shelby studied the ads for a moment, then said, "How about three grand?"

"Wish I could, but that's too stiff."

"And the Libya? You figured it for nothing?"

"I didn't count it at all. I can't use it. You hang onto it."

"From twenty-five thousand to twenty-five hundred . . . boy, what a beating."

"Twenty-four hundred," I corrected.

"Tell you what," he said, smiling, pointing at the album with two fingers that held a Winston. "Make it twenty-five hundred and you've got a deal."

I hesitated.

"Twenty-five hundred's a nice round figure. Ten percent of what I'd hoped to get. I know I got more than that in it."

"Okay, twenty-five hundred," I said. I reached into my attaché case for a check.

"What should I do with the Libya?"

"About the only thing you can do is keep it and hope you can sell it someday."

He tucked the Libyan stamps carefully back into the manila envelope and said, "Guess I know what they mean by 'Don't take any wooden nickels.'"

I chuckled.

"Thanks for coming all this way," Shelby said, as I walked back to my car with the Japanese album under my arm. "Have a safe trip back now, hear!"

And I did.

Chapter 13

The trip to Billings, Montana, had been a strange one, and I was glad to be leaving. That thought crossed my mind as Mike Moss dropped me off at the Billings airport. Once inside the terminal, it took only a minute to reach the United Airlines gate. The waiting area was deserted. A single Boeing 727 waited on the apron outside the terminal. I handed my ticket to the agent.

"Denver," she said, looking at the ticket. "Why don't you hold onto that for a little while."

"Is there a problem? Is the plane leaving on time?"

"I think so . . . if we get one more person." She smiled and handed the ticket back to me.

"What do you mean?"

"Sometimes the pilot doesn't make the trip if there's only one passenger on the flight."

"Are you serious?"

"Yes," she said, "why don't you have a seat over there. We have reservations for two more people. You're the first to show up. The others will probably be along shortly."

"You mean if they don't show up, we don't fly?"

"It's the pilot's decision," she said. "Sometimes he goes, sometimes he doesn't."

I wasn't sure I believed her. I assumed the plane had to return to Denver, if for no other reason than to maintain the schedule. I walked to the waiting area, sat down, and reflected on what a strange trip it had been. I had no desire to spend another night in Billings.

*   *   *

"How big is your collection?" I asked Moss the first time he phoned.

"Catalogue value's roughly four hundred thousand," Moss said. "I got Columbians, Omahas, Zepps, all the key stuff. I got foreign, too—good France, Swiss, British Commonwealth, Germany, lots of collections."

"Is the U.S. collection mint or used?"

"Both—mint *and* used." His tone seemed to imply, "Doesn't everyone?"

"How about condition?"

"Pretty standard, got most of it at auction." He rattled off the names of several well known auction houses.

"What are the key countries?"

"They're all pretty solid. Nice run of Swiss. France is good. Lots of British Commonwealth, including better stamps like Canada Jubilees—that kind of stuff. Like I said, there's lots of stamps here." His voice sounded mildly impatient, as if he wasn't used to being questioned.

"How does the value breaks down?"

"Well, the U.S. is worth more than a hundred and fifty grand by itself. The rest is spread out over the other albums. The British Commonwealth catalogues nearly a hundred grand."

"How much do you want for it?"

"I figure it ought to be worth a hundred grand—easily. There's a lot of good stuff here. You'll see what I mean when you get here."

"Have any other dealers looked at it?"

"Yeah." He paused.

"But you didn't sell?"

"No, they low-balled me."

Uh-oh, I thought, *the collection isn't worth what he wants for it.*

"That was about three years ago, before I had my heart attack. At the time, I wasn't in a hurry to get rid of it, but now, what with the heart attack and all, it's time to sell."

Moss's comments about the previous offer made me uncomfortable. On the other hand, he sounded motivated to sell. His asking price wasn't too far out of line if the collection proved to be as good as he said it was. From the way he talked, I concluded that he was a serious collector who had spent significant money building the collection. I decided it was worth a trip.

"Okay, I'll come up and take a look at it."

"Great!" he said. "I'll meet you at the airport."

Billings, Montana, is several hundred miles from Denver, but only about an hour by air. I was surprised to learn that United Airlines flew full-sized jets to Billings. I couldn't imagine there would be enough traffic to justify it. On the flight up, half a dozen other passengers and I had the plane to ourselves. It was a welcome change of pace from the habitually crowded flights to New York, Chicago, and Los Angeles. I planned to spend the afternoon looking at Moss's collection, then fly back the next day. At the time, only one flight a day connected Denver with Billings.

The flight arrived shortly after noon. A smiling Mike Moss greeted me, energetically shook my hand, and slapped me on the back as we made our way out of the terminal. Moss, sixtyish, balding, and slim, brimmed with nervous energy.

"Put your stuff back here," he said, opening the trunk of his big Cadillac whose mirror-like black finish gleamed in the winter sun. Twin red-and-white "Eat Beef" bumper stickers flanked the rear license plate.

On the way to his house, Moss pointed out local landmarks with the singular chest-swelling pride of a small-town chamber of commerce booster.

"There's the Prize Bull," he said, as we zoomed by a nondescript restaurant sitting behind a dusty parking lot. "Smitty owns it. Best steaks in town . . . I oughta know," he said, glancing over at me with his wide-as-the-Montana-sky smile, "He gets 'em from me. You'll see, we'll eat there tonight."

I nodded and smiled politely.

"There's Lorraine's," he said, as we passed a mousey looking storefront with a large sign that read, "The Clippe Joynte."

"Wife gets her hair done there."

We hit the edge of town and flew by miles of brown flatland.

"You mentioned you were in ranching?" I said, trying to be conversational.

"Sort of. Might say I'm more of a broker these days. The real money's in buying and selling," he said, looking over at me with a knowing, crafty smile. "Yes, sir. Wheelin' and dealin' . . . that's the name of the game."

Mike Moss gave me a ten-minute lesson in the cattle business, punctuating his comments by pointing as we passed things he thought might interest me.

The Mosses lived in a modest brick ranch home set back about a quarter of a mile from the road. A freshly painted white fence demarcated a well manicured yard from the surrounding rangeland. A few head of cattle grazed in the distance.

"Home sweet home," Moss said, as we pulled up. He rolled to a stop, shifted into park, released his seat belt, opened the door, and was out of the car in one swift, synchronized movement. He retrieved my overnight bag and attaché case from the trunk and we headed for the front door.

"I'd like you to meet my wife, Amanda," he said as we entered the house.

"How do you do?" Mrs. Moss said, extending her hand. "Won't you please come in?" I stepped in, and Moss breezed by me, barely stopping to greet his wife before heading through the kitchen to a flight of linoleum-covered stairs.

"The stamps are in the basement," he said. "Might as well get to it." He flipped on the basement light and descended the stairs. I followed. The bottom of the stairs opened into a long spacious room containing a ping-pong table, a pool table, a sofa, and half a dozen large, overstuffed, maroon vinyl-covered chairs clustered around a circular split-pine coffee table. At the far end of the room, on the wall behind the bar, a neon sign boldly announced: "Schlitz Served Here!" A red garter belt dangled from the left tip of a pair of steer horns hung next to the Schlitz sign. Fishing trophies crowded the other walls, including one I took to be a marlin or a swordfish. An expensive-looking exercise bike was parked near one end of the ping-pong table. The shelves behind the ping-pong table sagged under the weight of dozens of stamp albums.

"Ever see a collection this big?" Moss asked, gesturing toward the wall of stamps.

"It's impressive," I said. I had seen larger collections, even bought larger collections, but saw no reason to mention it.

"You can work right here," he said, pulling the string that switched on the florescent lamp above the ping-pong table. "There's plenty of room." Moss tugged the first album from the end of the lowest shelf. I retrieved stamp tongs, calculator, and a yellow legal pad from my attaché case.

As I worked, Moss prowled restlessly around the room. He shot a little pool, then introduced me to some of his fishing trophies. "Caught that baby off Mazatlán . . . helluva fighter . . . damn fine trophy."

I didn't pay much attention to him. I couldn't afford to; I had dozens of albums to go through and limited time in which to do it. Moss didn't seem to mind my preoccupation. He just kept talking.

The foreign albums were a disappointment. They were heavily loaded with faulty nineteenth century stamps, the kind notorious for high catalogue prices but low market values. About the time I reached the first U.S. album, Moss climbed onto the exercise bike and turned it on. Mechanically, rhythmically, his feet pumped up and down; his arms rowed forward and backward. He increased the speed until his arms and legs moved with the briskness of a racing athlete, yet the bike went nowhere. The effect was slightly comical. I stifled a chuckle.

"Ever since the heart attack, Doc says I got to use this damn thing every day. What the hell, I guess it's good for me."

He pedaled along, watching my progress and chatting. "I think you got the mint album there. See the Columbians yet?" he asked, craning his neck as it jerked back and forth in a motion that looked like the kind a chicken's neck makes when it walks.

I flipped through the front section of the U.S. album until I found the Columbians. The set was complete. One by one, I pulled them out of their mounts, quickly checking for faults. The $5 value was regummed over a closed tear. The $4 value, sound but also regummed. The $3 value, fresh and lovely, but thinned and without gum. The $2 value, original gum but also thinned and terribly off center. I didn't bother to check the dollar value. Spot checking the Trans-Mississippis revealed the same miserable condition. I began to get a sinking feeling.

"Nice stuff, huh?" Moss said, pedalling energetically.

"Well, you do have all the key stamps," I said, "But condition is pretty poor—thins, creases, regums, reperfs."

"Hell, most old stamps are like that," he snorted.

"From what you said on the phone, I expected a better grade of stamps. The keys are uniformly faulty."

"I got these stamps from big-name dealers and auctions," he said as if surprised by my remarks.

"Well, it looks to me like you bought seconds and remainders. Even the biggest auctions sell remainders and bulk collections. You can always find impaired material at reasonable prices. I'd just hoped for better quality," I said with a sigh. Then, "Let me get back to work and see what I come up with." It wouldn't accomplish anything to waste time arguing. Had it been a local call, I could have wrapped it up quickly and left. Since I had to stay the night, I decided to take my time on the chance that the numbers might approach his asking price.

My remarks displeased Moss. He scowled and pedaled silently, gripping the handlebars of the motorized bike until his knuckles turned white.

I worked through the massive collection. It catalogued at least as much as he had estimated, but it was full of off-quality material—clunkers. Even the later sets, such as Farleys and famous Americans, were hinged. By the end of the afternoon, I knew I couldn't meet his price.

"All done," I announced, closing the last album. While I had worked, Moss finished his bike ride, made a few phone calls, shot some more pool, and gotten his good humor back.

"What did you come up with?" he asked, setting his pool cue down, walking over to the ping-pong table.

"As I mentioned, the overall condition of your stamps isn't what I'd expected. You said you wanted a hundred thousand for the lot?"

"Right."

"I don't think I can meet your figure."

Moss grimaced.

"But before I do make an offer, I'd like to think about it overnight."

Moss started to speak, paused for a second as if thinking better of it, then said magnanimously, "Sure, why not. Say, how about a drink?"

"That would taste good right about now," I said, replacing tongs, legal pad, and calculator in my attaché case.

Moss led the way upstairs and said, "Mandy, how about a drink for Steve and me."

"My goodness, is it five o'clock already?" she said cordially. "I'll bet you fellas *are* thirsty. What can I get for you, Mr. Datz?"

"Gin and tonic would be fine, if you've got it."

"We've got everything," Moss said, snickering as if amused by the thought that he might not have something someone requested. Over drinks, I learned that Mrs. Moss had a slight in interest stamps. She had formed several topical collections including flowers—she loved to garden—and a Disney collection for her grandchildren. Mrs. Moss was a pleasant conversationalist and a gracious hostess. Chatting with her—despite her husband's energetic interruptions—put me at ease. I soon forgot about the collection that lurked in the basement.

At 5:30, we headed for the Prize Bull. Moss wheeled the big black Cadillac into a parking space near the front entrance. I noticed only three other parked cars. Apparently, Tuesday evening wasn't a big night for dining out in Billings.

It had grown dark and chilly outside. The wind had come up. It bit my face as I stepped out of the Cadillac and sent an empty Pepsi can skittering across the parking lot behind me. Moss pushed open the door. Mrs. Moss and I hurried in.

"Three for dinner?" the hostess asked.

"That's right, sweetheart," Moss said smiling at the young woman. "Our usual table."

"Sure thing, Mr. Moss." She seated us in a large booth midway back.

"Smitty in tonight?" Moss asked.

"Sure is."

"Be a real sweetheart and let him know I'm here, would you?"

"Sure thing."

"Best restaurant in town," Moss said, as she walked away. "You're gonna love the steaks."

Within minutes, a waitress had taken our drink orders and served us a relish tray of celery, carrots, and broccoli arranged around a cup of ranch dressing.

"Are you going to take the collection back to Denver with you?" Mrs. Moss asked.

"Perhaps," I said. "If we make a deal."

"Oh, we'll make a deal," Moss said. Then to me, "C'mon Steve, admit it. You don't see collections like mine every day, do you?"

"No, you don't," I answered diplomatically, seeing no purpose in bursting Moss's bubble in front of his wife.

"Probably the best collection in the state," he said, taking a decisive bite on a stalk of celery.

"Could be," I said, and perhaps it was. There couldn't be too many other collections in Montana. Moss smiled, taking my remark as a bona fide compliment.

About that time, a large pot-bellied man who resembled W.C. Fields approached the table and said, "Out on the town tonight, Mike?"

"Yup, and we've got a man from Colorado here. Promised to show him what a *real* steak's like. You can handle that, can't you?"

"I think so," the big man chuckled.

Moss turned to me and asked, "What's your pleasure? Prime rib? T-bone? New York strip?"

"New York strip, medium rare," I said.

"Sure you wouldn't like to try the prime rib? It'll melt in your mouth. You'll never taste better," Moss pressed.

"New York strip will be fine."

"Fix Steve up with the best cut you've got, hear?" Moss said to Smitty, who seemed to enjoy Moss's performance. I wasn't sure if Moss was trying to impress me, Smitty, or just loved to hear himself talk.

Moss tried to order a T-bone, but Mrs. Moss put her foot down. "Mike, you know what the doctor said."

Moss looked crestfallen. "Okay, okay. Halibut steak, hold the butter."

Smitty chuckled and walked back to the kitchen. We ate our salads, then the main course arrived.

"What did I tell you? Damn fine steak, huh?" Moss said as I took my first bite. I nodded. Surprisingly, the steak was excellent. I'd been leery, suspecting his build-up of the steak to be as exaggerated as his build-up of the stamp collection. I decided Moss was a better judge of steaks than stamps.

Moss savaged the halibut like a predator on a fresh kill. He cajoled Mrs. Moss into giving him a bite of her prime rib, which he savored for a long moment with eyes closed. When we had finished dinner, he left a big tip, calling the waitress's attention to the size of it. He waved goodbye to Smitty who peered out from the kitchen. "Damn fine meal, Smitty!" he said. Smitty smiled and waved back.

"I booked a room for you at the MGM Grand," Moss said as we got into the Cadillac. "It's only a couple blocks from here."

He wheeled the big car out of the Prize Bull's lot and headed down the deserted, windy street. When he said MGM Grand, I visualized the hotel by the same name in Reno, but I should have known better. It turned out to be an aging motel built in the 1930s or 1940s, the kind they used to call motor courts. The name "MGM Grand" had been inserted in big blue plastic letters on a sign that looked like a theater marquee. Below the motel's name, the word "Vacancy" appeared in smaller letters. A solitary spotlight illuminated the sign. The MGM Grand's dozen rooms opened directly onto the parking lot. Moss pulled up to the door of one and shoved the shift lever into park.

"Here's your key," he said. "And don't worry, the bill's been taken care of."

Then he said, "There's not much in the way of TV up here, so I brought along a little something I thought you might get a kick out of." He handed me a stamp album. "Mandy and I like to work on this on cold winter evenings when there's nothing else to do. It's sort of a topical collection. We've had a lot of fun thinking up the captions—haven't we honey?" he said, looking at his wife in the back seat.

"It *has* amused us," she admitted.

"Anyway, you enjoy it, and I'll pick you up at eight tomorrow morning. That's not too early is it?"

"No, that'll be fine. And thanks for dinner."

"Don't mention it. Just because we live out in the boondocks doesn't mean we don't know how to treat company. Enjoy the collection, and I'll see you at eight in the morning."

"Thanks again," I said as I climbed out of the car.

The big black Cadillac backed up with a lurch, swung around, and stopped for an instant under the MGM Grand sign while Moss checked for oncoming traffic. The street was deserted. Moss punched it, tires squealed, and the Cadillac sped off into the night.

The motel room was as plain and unpretentious as the Montana rangeland. I sat on the bed, propped up a pillow, and began to page through the album Moss had left with me. It was a topical collection of nudes, including everything from Spain's Goya nude to Paraguayan and Gulf States reproductions of Rubens, Renoir, and Modigliani paintings. Comic strip bubbles had been drawn above each stamp as if the central characters were speaking.

Spain's Goya nude said, "Why don't ya come up and see me sometime?"

In another, two Rubens nudes looked as if they were sharing a secret. A eunuch with a scimitar stood in the background. The bubble read, "Looks like a nice guy, but I've heard he's travelling light."

I read and laughed, read and laughed, until my eyes were moist. Then, I slept.

Mike Moss showed up promptly at eight the next morning.

"How did you like the X-rated collection?" he asked as we pulled out of the MGM Grand's parking lot. He was in a great mood.

"I've never seen another like it. Does it go with the deal?"

"I hadn't thought about it, but, sure, I suppose it could."

I'd pondered Moss's collection overnight and decided he would have to settle for a much lower price or there would be no deal. The more I had thought about the marginal condition of the collection, the less it appealed to me.

Mandy Moss served me toast, bacon, and orange juice when we arrived. She served Moss a bowl of oatmeal. "I don't see how anybody can live on this stuff," he grumbled.

After breakfast, we adjourned to the basement. Moss busied himself at the phone, then rode his motorized exercise bike while I looked through the albums again. In the cold light of the new day, the collection had lost its appeal. I saw it for what it was, a vast accumulation of faulty stamps made marginally impressive only by sheer bulk and scope. The funny thing about buying collections is that, in the heat of negotiations, there's great motivation to close a deal. Later, the sense of urgency disappears and other thoughts, such as *How am I going to market this?* sink in. Experience teaches that collections never look as appealing on subsequent inspections as they do the first time around. Suddenly, with the stamps in front of me, I was less inclined to offer as much as I had considered offering the day before.

"What do you think?" Moss asked when I had finished.

"It's not worth a hundred thousand."

"It catalogues more than four hundred thousand!"

"True—but based on the 1981 catalogue. That was three years ago, and the market's come way down since then."

Moss climbed off the exercise bike and sat on the end of the ping-pong table. "Okay, so it's come down a little. I'm not unreasonable. I can be flexible if that's what it takes to make a deal. How about eighty thousand?"

I didn't say anything.

"That's a helluva price," Moss said in his best salesman's voice.

"Besides the fact that the catalogue value's come down," I said, "I have another problem with the collection—quality. If the quality were uniformly better, your price wouldn't be unreasonable. But all the expensive keys are faulty—I didn't see any that weren't."

"So, what's your offer," he said, his tone suddenly frosty with impatience.

"Thirty-five thousand."

"That's not even a tenth of catalogue!"

"It's more than a tenth. Your figures are based on 1981 prices. If you'd used the current catalogue, the collection would total less—probably around three hundred twenty-five thousand.

Besides, that's not the issue.   Condition is what's killing the collection."

"Yeah, I've heard that before," he said sarcastically.   "Same thing that dealer from New York said."

"Well, it's true—"

"You know what really gets me?   You guys charge an arm and a leg for this stuff, then when it's time to sell, you knock the condition and act like it's worthless.   That guy from New York figured he'd knock my stamps, then get 'em for a song.   Well, I told him where to go."

His attitude annoyed me.

"You know what you paid for these stamps and so do I," I shot back, motioning to the wall full of albums.   "You know perfectly well what the market for faulty stamps is.   You bought bargains at bargain prices—probably ten to fifteen percent of catalogue.   What makes you think I'm going to pay twenty-five percent for material I can buy for ten or fifteen percent at the same auctions?"

He didn't react.   I knew I had hit the nail on the head.

"You've made a long trip," he said in a calculated tone, the confrontational hardness gone from his voice.   "Be a shame for you to go home empty handed."

"It wouldn't be the first time."   He didn't seem to understand that I wasn't going to pay $80,000 for his collection.

"Thirty-five thousand is a reasonable price.   I'll write you a check right now," I said, taking a check from my attaché case.   "Cash in hand is better than a collection whose value is uncertain in a falling market."

He smiled.   "Make it seventy-five thousand, and you've got a deal."

"At thirty-five thousand, I'm a buyer.   At seventy-five, I'm not.   Thirty-five is the best I can do."

"It's going to take seventy-five to get me to part with it," he said calmly.

"Well then, you're going to have to find someone else.   I can't stay in business paying more for stamps than they're worth."

"I've been talking to an outfit in San Francisco," he said.   "They didn't seem to think my price was out of line."

"They haven't seen the stamps yet. They're assuming the stamps are sound—just like I did. After they've seen them, they'll tell you the same thing." I looked him directly in the eye to emphasize the point. He didn't say anything, then looked away. He knew I was right.

I realized there would be no deal. Moss would continue to shop the collection around as long as dealers were willing to fly in to view it. I knew that no one would meet his asking price. Unfortunately, he didn't know it yet.

"We're too far apart," I said, gathering my pad and calculator. "We're not going to be able to get together."

"Seventy," he said.

"No, I mean it. It's not a matter of dickering. The gap's too great. Thirty-five is as high as I'm prepared to go."

"Hate to see you leave without the collection," he said. "You don't want to waste a trip do you?"

"Sometimes you have to. I've made a fair offer. There's nothing more I can do."

Moss studied me for a moment, then slid off the end of the ping-pong table and stood. "Okay, I'll give you a lift to the airport." And that was that.

All I had to show for my trip to Billings was a question mark about whether I would get back to Denver that day. I knew from experience that you don't buy every collection you go after, and I didn't feel bad about leaving this one. I just wanted to get back to Denver.

Finally, the pilot and co-pilot strolled up to the ticket agent. After exchanging remarks with her, they set their bags down behind the counter and went off somewhere. Pilots usually go right onto the plane. I wondered if there would be a flight. *Last time I ever come to Billings,* I thought. *It'll be just my luck that no one else shows up, and I'll be stuck for another night at the MGM Grand.*

I almost jumped for joy when, at long last, a man and a woman carrying luggage appeared. They produced tickets and checked their luggage. When they had finished, the agent motioned to me.

"Looks like a go," she said, as I approached the counter. She removed the ticket stub, placed it in the ticket jacket, and handed it back to me. She hadn't marked a seat assignment on the jacket.

"Sit wherever you like," she said, smiling. "I don't think you'll have a problem."

I chose a window seat midway down the aisle. The man and woman—the only other passengers on the flight—sat across the aisle and forward. I settled back into my seat as the plane climbed to altitude. I craned my neck to see if I could spot Moss's place, but I couldn't locate it on the brown Montana rangeland that spread as far as the eye could see.

Helluva long trip to make for a steak dinner, I thought, and it amused me, as did the MGM Grand Motel and the X-rated stamp collection.

Chapter 14

No matter what your business, getting away from the grind has a rejuvenating effect. Some dealers like to arrive early at shows and spend time lounging near a swimming pool or on the ski slopes. I enjoy driving, being alone in the car away from the office, the telephone, and the pressures of business.

It was sunny and unseasonably warm the late October morning I left Denver for Albuquerque, New Mexico, perfect driving weather for a buying trip. Albuquerque lies 450 miles south of Denver, about a nine-hour drive. I had three definite appointments and a couple of maybes. I felt confident that I would buy at least one collection, with a little luck, perhaps all three.

South of Colorado Springs there was little traffic, and south of Raton Pass, none at all. It seemed that the farther south I drove, the larger the cloudless sky and the farther away the horizon. The hours passed quickly, and I reached Albuquerque by five o'clock. I checked into a motel on the interstate and called to confirm my appointments for the next day, jotting street directions to individual destinations.

My first appointment took me out in the country. Billy Masterson's Airstream trailer was right where he said it would be. At least, I assumed I had the right address; there were no other dwellings in sight. I pulled off the road, down a dusty driveway, and parked next to a battered 1950s vintage Ford pickup truck. The aluminum-finish trailer sat like the centerpiece in an accumulation of clutter: vehicle parts, rusted machine parts, fence posts, firewood, tangled barbed wire, weathered signs, and myriad odds and ends.

Masterson, fiftyish, had brushcut hair and wore a T-shirt and blue jeans held up by wide olive-drab suspenders. He watched me from the door of the Airstream. As I got out of the car, he pushed the screen door open and stepped down, saying, "You must be the stamp man." He moved with a slight limp, as if his hip bothered him.

"That's right," I said, suddenly feeling overdressed in my suit and tie.

"Hope you didn't have any trouble finding me."

"Not a bit. Your directions were just fine." Masterson's trailer would have been difficult to miss. There was nothing else for miles around.

"Come on in," he said, "I'll show you what I got."

I stepped up into the trailer. A small, scruffy dog the size of a terrier pranced around, wagging its stump of a tail, sniffing at my leg.

"Lucky, leave the man alone," Masterson said, his tone that of a parent gently reminding a child of its manners. "That's my little buddy, Lucky," he said. Lucky didn't pay much attention to Masterson and continued to sniff at my pants and attaché case.

"Have a seat," he said, motioning toward a formica-covered, metal-rimmed table. "I'll get the stamps." He rummaged around in a closet.

A dried, stretched rattlesnake skin adorned the wall across from the table. Next to it, a crucifix. Farther down, a framed black-and-white gag photo of Billy in his younger days, rifle in hand, standing proudly next to his hunting trophy, the mythical jackalope, a cross between a pronghorn antelope and a jack rabbit. The faint sound of a country-western ballad emanated from an old radio on the counter near the sink.

"I stuck it in the back of the closet for safekeeping," Masterson grunted, as he tugged the carton out from under a pile of clothes. Finally, it came free. He tossed a couple shirts and socks from atop the box back into the closet and scooted it toward the table.

"Belonged to my brother," he said. "He died last year and left me the stamps. I know zilch about stamps, but according to the adding machine tapes in the albums, they're pretty good."

Masterson had mentioned a catalogue value of $15,000 when he had called. When he had finished pushing the box to the table, he slid into the seat across from me. Lucky hopped onto his lap, and Masterson absentmindedly scratched the little dog behind the ears as he spoke.

"Disability payments don't seem to go very far these days, and the stamps don't mean nothin' to me, so I figured I might as well cash 'em in."

I opened the first album and began looking. Masterson continued talking.

"I served in Korea, then mined uranium back when the boom was on. The money was good, until I got hurt. I'm on disability now. It ain't much, but me and Lucky get by. Don't we, boy?" The dog looked up at him, then returned its gaze to me. Masterson continued gently massaging the dog's neck.

I quickly looked through the collection to get an idea of its scope. It was primarily a topical collection: a couple albums devoted to Boy Scouts, a couple more to religion, a couple to music, and a few others for containing multiple topics such as flowers, birds, animals, etc.

Masterson's brother had concentrated on complete mint sets. The best part of the collection appeared to have been formed in the 1950s and 1960s. From what I could tell, he had bought the stamps as new issues. Masterson's brother had pursued his topics diligently. The music albums contained the German Wagner set of 1934, the Berlin bells, and postwar German and Austrian composers, among others. The religious topic contained the Belgian Mercier issue, the India Gandhi issue, and the Argentine airmail semi-postal Pieta. The Boy Scout topic included all the better items, such as the Cyprus souvenir sheet.

Masterson's brother had carefully mounted the collection on cream-colored construction-paper pages, then arranged the pages by topic in non-matching three-ring binders that had been salvaged from one source or another. Early on, the brother had used a typewriter for write-ups. Later, he had switched to ballpoint pen, pressing heavily, leaving deep ruts in the soft construction paper. He had made numerous erasures and, in some cases, liberally used white correction fluid, which looked unsightly against the cream color of the pages. The combined effect of erasures and correction fluid gave the pages the appearance of having open sores and deep scars.

Masterson's brother had used sleeve-type mounts that, when attached vertically on pages, allowed stamps to slip out the bottom. To solve the problem he had taped both tops and bottoms shut, often heavily. Over the years, the tape had turned brown, discoloring stamps wherever it touched them.

The few that escaped being taped appeared to stay magically in place. Sadly, when I tested them with tongs, I discovered they were stuck down, the result of too much saliva being applied to the backs of the mounts. Besides the stuck-down stamps, others were crimped from having been mounted in plastic sleeves too tight for them.

Perhaps in his later years, Masterson's brother had suffered from arthritis or some other affliction that impaired his manual dexterity, or so it appeared, because his mounting became increasingly sloppy, his handwriting cruder. Open tops and bottoms of later mounts had been haphazardly taped directly to album pages. At some point, he had given up mounts altogether and simply hinged his latest acquisitions with Scotch tape. Toward the end, he had added notes throughout the albums—perhaps to aid his brother Billy. The notes, such as "This is a good set," had been scrawled unevenly next to selected items.

In terms of condition, it was the worst collection I had ever seen. That is to say, I had never seen so many stamps, presumably acquired in sound condition, ruined by such pervasive thoughtless handling. The collection was like a concentration camp for stamps.

The German Wagner set had been never-hinged before being mounted. Now, some values were stained, others stuck down by excess saliva. In an attempt to protect his stamps, Masterson's brother had utterly destroyed them. It broke my heart.

Masterson was unaware of the problem. He had seen only the adding machine tapes and their tantalizing sum—$15,000. Unfortunately, the collection was virtually worthless due to its condition. It would be difficult to resell. I silently sighed.

"Your brother collected some excellent stamps," I began. Masterson smiled at the compliment. "But he was rather careless, shall we say, in the way he mounted and protected them."

Masterson's brow furrowed as if to say, "Oh?"

"Look," I said, opening an album to a random page and poking my stamp tongs into one mount after another to demonstrate how the stamps were stuck down. "Mounts are supposed to protect stamps, keep them like new because that's what collectors prize—perfect condition. I'm sorry to say, the stamps in this collection are all damaged."

Masterson listened glumly.

"Look at this one," I said, selecting a cheap stamp to make my point. I popped it out of its mount. "See how part of the stamp remains in the mount when you try to pull it out. The backside is now thinned." I held the stamp out so he could see for himself.

He looked at it, saw the thin, but didn't seem to understand its significance.

"Collectors like perfect stamps—perfect centering, perfect gum, perfect color. Your stamps . . . well, they're in bad shape."

"What are you saying? That these stamps aren't worth anything?"

"No, they're not worthless, but nearly so."

Masterson's eyes narrowed, his face hardened.

"You've got stamps hinged with tape, stamps stained by tape, stamps crimped by undersized mounts, stamps stuck inside mounts."

Masterson put his hand to his face and drew it down over his chin.

If only the brother had left the stamps in glassines when he'd bought them, Masterson would get a decent price, and I'd get a worthwhile collection.

"It's like old cars," I said. "A cream puff in like-new condition might be worth $10,000. The very same car, not running, rusted out, a literal pile of junk, might be worth only a couple hundred dollars. It's all a matter of condition. Same way with stamps."

The automobile analogy seemed to make sense to him, because he appeared to relax. He resumed scratching Lucky behind the ears.

"And my stamps ain't all that great?"

"That's right."

"Well, they don't look too bad to me."

"Well, I don't make the rules. I'm just telling you how it is. Collectors are very particular about condition. It's tough to sell stamps with stains, thins, those kinds of problems—and that's a fact."

"So, what are they worth?"

The figure was so low, I dreaded having to tell him. I toyed with the idea of avoiding the issue altogether, of just thanking him and leaving. But, since I had made the trip, I decided to try to salvage something out of it. I punched the keys on my calculator. I wanted to know how much two-and-a-half percent of $15,000 was.

"Three hundred seventy-five dollars," I said.

"Jesus Christ!" Masterson half-gasped, half-exclaimed, "That's nothin'!"

"Look, you're welcome to keep it." I didn't want to rile him any further.

"Excuse me, mister, but I just don't understand all this nit-picking. I got tapes here adding up to fifteen thousand, and you come waltzing in and tell me I'm not even gonna get a dime on the dollar. I may be a country boy, but my Momma didn't raise no fools."

"I'd be upset, too, if I were in your place. All I can say is that I'm not trying to pull a fast one. Collections like this are really tough to sell, so it won't break my heart if you decide to keep it."

"Some deal," he exhaled loudly. Lucky lowered his ears, perhaps thinking he had displeased his master.

I decided it was time to go. I replaced my tongs, calculator, note pad and pen in my attaché case and snapped it shut.

"I wasn't trying to insult you. I was just trying to tell you the way it is. Maybe the next guy will offer you more. But if you're waiting to get fifteen grand, or five grand, or even a thousand, don't hold your breath."

I started to slide out of the nook.

"Hold on a minute," Masterson said. "I want to sell the collection . . . I just don't want to get taken."

"Like I said, I'm not trying to pull your leg. I told you what the stamps are worth to me. If you want to sell, that's fine—if not, why that's okay, too. It makes no difference to me."

"Would you go five hundred?" he asked.

"Four hundred," I countered.

"Four hundred! Jesus, you're practically stealing it the way it is . . . and me and Lucky could sure use the money." He smiled and patted Lucky, who panted happily and looked like he wanted to hop over the table and into my lap. "How about four-fifty?"

I paused, then knew I couldn't argue. "Okay, four-fifty," I said, not knowing why.

"That's mighty nice of you," Masterson said. "Me and Lucky sure appreciate it, don't we, boy?" He glanced down at the dog, which reached up as if to lick him on the chin.

"Say thank you to the man," he urged the dog. "Go on, say thank you."

Lucky yarked, looking pleased with himself. I wrote out a check, wondering if I had lost my mind.

"Lucky likes you," Masterson said as I wrote.

When I extended my arm to hand Masterson the check, Lucky put his front feet on the table, reaching for the piece of paper—or maybe my hand.

"No, no, Lucky," Masterson said. "That's not good to eat, but it'll sure buy a lot of doggie biscuits." Lucky yarked and I chuckled.

I slid to the edge of my seat and began repacking the albums in the carton. Lucky hopped off Masterson's lap and, wagging his stump of a tail, sniffed around the carton while I worked.

"Nice dog," I said, patting his head. If dogs could smile, Lucky would have smiled at me.

"Like I said, Lucky likes you."

"He's a good little dog," I said. "You be sure to get him a bone."

Masterson stood, and Lucky pranced around his feet. "Don't you worry. We're gonna crank up the old Ford, run into town, cash this check, and get us both something special. Huh, boy?"

Masterson held the screen door open for me. Lucky followed me out to the car. For a moment, I thought he might jump in.

"C'mon back, boy," Masterson hollered, patting his leg. "C'mon." Lucky raced back to the door of the Airstream and hopped up the steps.

I loaded the carton. The morning sun, warm and bright, glinted on the Airstream. I removed my suit coat and hung it carefully on the hook behind the driver's seat, then got in and waved goodbye to Masterson. I steered the car in a circle, careful to avoid the clutter, pulled out onto the road, and headed back to Albuquerque.

Chapter 15

In terms of condition, Billy Masterson's brother's collection was the worst I had ever seen. Back in my motel room, as I looked through it a second time, I remembered the best collection I'd ever seen. Edson Chapman had meticulously mounted his tens of thousands of stamps in clear mylar mounts.

Chapman was in his late seventies when I first met him. He lived in a quietly elegant neighborhood, in a single-floor ranch dwelling of several thousand square feet with a semi-circular front drive.

"Please excuse the door," he said, as if worried that I might find the ornate iron security gate that protected his front door in poor taste, "I was burglarized recently." He unlocked it, and I stepped into an impeccably decorated home. It looked like something out of *Architectural Digest*.

He led me into his study, devoted almost entirely to stamps. Bookshelves lined the walls. An oversized desk, which was perfectly positioned to take advantage of the light, occupied a corner near the study's large window.

"Because of the burglary," Chapman said, after we had exchanged pleasantries, "I've decided to sell." He wore neatly pressed tan slacks, a blue Oxford cloth shirt, a muted maroon tie, and a dark blue sweater vest. His thin, grey-white hair was combed straight back. "I'm afraid to keep the stamps anymore. I surprised the burglars the afternoon they broke in," he said quietly, earnestly. He sat absolutely upright, like a West Point cadet.

"As I came in the front door, they were going out a back window—the same one they'd broken to get in. They fled when they heard me unlock the front door."

He rose and pushed aside sliding closet doors. A large black safe occupied the center space, to the left, shelves of albums; to the right, an open space. Mr. Chapman reached into the open space and pulled out an old double-barreled shotgun.

"It was loaded," he said, holding the shotgun up for me to see. "They were trying to get into the safe when I came home. The gun was right there. They could have picked it up and blown me to Kingdom Come. Thank God, they didn't." He replaced the shotgun in the closet.

I nodded, thinking he was, indeed, lucky. The intruders could have been high on drugs, could have shot him without a second thought.

"Now, I've got an iron security door, a burglar alarm, and I worry every time I leave the house. If I hadn't come home when I did, they would have gotten away with the stamps. Anyway, the time has come to think about selling.

"You can work right here on the desk," he said. The desk was Spartan: an old visored lamp, a green felt blotter, a calculator, a wooden cup holding pens and pencils, and heavy crystal paper-weight containing a magnificent chrome-yellow butterfly. I'd never seen a more beautiful butterfly.

I began looking through the albums, checking for hinging and condition.

"The stamps are mostly never hinged," Chapman said.

"Just doing some spot checking to satisfy my curiosity," I replied. Dealers are eternal skeptics.

Album followed album, until I thought they would never end. The collection contained all the key modern sets, the sets dealers always hope to find but know better than to expect. The Austrian Dollfuss 10 schilling stamp, the Netherlands airmail gulls, the Spanish submarines, the Croatia storm trooper souvenir sheet, a complete run of French Southern and Antarctic Territories issues, and many more.

Most collections are predictably mediocre, runs of the same old common stamps, keys few and far between. But not the Chapman collection. He had it all. For almost forty years, Edson Chapman had diligently purchased new issues for nearly every country in the world except those in South America. He had also filled spaces for earlier issues going back to about 1920. Occasionally, one of the earlier stamps was lightly hinged—but never with more than the barest trace of a hinge mark.   Chapman had ignored nineteenth century issues, concentrating, instead, on twentieth century stamps. Appealing, colorful sets, the kind that first began to proliferate in the 1930s, packed every album. It was the finest collection of mint stamps from the Golden Age of Philately I had ever seen, and all highly salable.

"Every album's catalogued," Chapman said, producing a notebook thick with adding machine tapes neatly folded and paper clipped to summary pages. I wasn't surprised. Everything about Edson Chapman—his home, his clothing, his desk, the way he mounted his collection—suggested a highly organized person.

"Great, that'll save a lot of time," I said as he handed me the notebook opened to the first page. I looked through it, comparing country totals to my estimates.

"I got a great deal of pleasure out of my stamps," he said as I worked. He spoke at a leisurely pace, like a meandering stream, yet he was careful to articulate his words precisely. "We never had children, and I was never much interested in TV. I enjoyed spending evenings working on the collection. Great way to relax.

"I always felt I owed a lot to stamps," he said. "Stamps taught me names of places most people have never heard of—Mozambique, Kiauchau, Bosnia and Herzegovina, Carpatho-Ukraine.

"And history—wars, revolutions, nations being born and nations disappearing from the map.

"And great men and women—Molly Pitcher, the Curies, Captain Cook, and dozens of others. Much of what I know about the world I learned from stamps, perhaps as much I ever learned from reading."

His words struck a familiar chord. I, too, shared the experience of learning from stamps. I remember amazing my history and geography teachers with bits of esoteric knowledge. I knew who Marshal Pilsudski was and when Latvia, Lithuania and Estonia disappeared from the map. I knew who William Stanton was and when Brazil gained independence. I knew who Napoleon III was and that balloons were used to fly mail out of besieged Paris during the Franco-Prussian War. I knew about German Southwest Africa and Manchukou and a host of other places and events that even my teachers were often not aware of—all from stamps.

Occasionally you wonder if you're the only one who's ever absorbed so much historical minutia and if it's really relevant to everyday life. Then you meet a man like Edson Chapman and realize that you're not alone. You realize that the knowledge is worthwhile because it gives you a better understanding of the world.

"I grew up in South Carolina," Chapman said. "Studied engineering, served in the Army, and moved to Colorado right after the war. I liked the climate here, the dry air."

He lacked a noticeable accent, but his demeanor and the way he spoke were that of a Southern gentleman.

"I was lucky and did well in business. Life has been generous to me," he said with genuine modesty.

I liked Edson Chapman. He impressed me as a bright, hard-working man, the kind who prides himself on doing his best, the kind people naturally trust and seek out. That's why he had done well in business. Luck had nothing to do with it.

He reminisced while I worked, calling my attention to one set or another. Often, collectors point out their most valuable stamps, Edson Chapman pointed out those that pleased him or had a personal tale behind them, even if the value was nominal.

"Czechoslovakian stamps have always been favorites of mine. The combination of the traditional—engraving—with the avant garde—style and color combinations—is striking and, to me, highly appealing. I've always suspected there are quite a few free spirits living there, despite the communist regime."

I realized that stamps meant a lot more to Edson Chapman than how much they had cost. Between stamps and conversation, time passed pleasantly. Before I knew it, most of the afternoon had slipped away. At least, I had finished valuing the albums.

I double-checked my figures. Stamps of some countries are worth greater percentages of catalogue value than others. I applied the appropriate percentage to each section and totaled the results. The time had come to talk business.

"I can offer eighty thousand dollars," I said.

Chapman flushed and didn't speak at first.

"You can't be serious," he said gravely. "The collection catalogues nearly four hundred thousand dollars!" Anger flashed in his eyes, but he didn't raise his voice.

I had been afraid this would happen. Catalogue prices are not market prices. That was especially true in 1984 at the time I made my offer to Edson Chapman. At the time, catalogue prices were far above market prices. The disparity made it difficult to buy collections, to appear credible to sellers. I had lost more than one deal when sellers, angered by what they perceived to be insultingly low offers, ended negotiations with the finality of a meat cleaver hitting a chopping block.

I reached into my attaché case for some clippings and auction catalogues to illustrate my point. Suspicion clouded his face.

"Look," I said, offering a full page newspaper ad from *Linn's Stamp News*. A bold headline across the top of the page read: "SELECTED WESTERN EUROPE AT UP TO 75 PERCENT OFF CATALOGUE" Another read: "GIGANTIC SAVINGS! SPECIALS AT ONE-THIRD SCOTT!"

"No one's selling at full catalogue. The real market is only a fraction of catalogue." I handed him a variety of New York auction catalogues with prices realized marked in the margins. "I can buy collections similar to yours—smaller, of course—for the percentages of catalogue indicated."

He scanned the newspaper advertisements and auction catalogues with a critical eye. Finally, he said in a calm but disappointed tone, "I had no idea there was such an enormous disparity between catalogue and market prices. It's a shock."

He pointed to the notebook containing the adding machine tapes. "You add up all your stamps, and assume you're going to get a significant sum. Then, to be told your stamps are worth only a fraction of what you thought they were worth . . ." He looked at me and shook his head slowly from side to side. "It's a shock."

"What had you hoped to get?" I asked.

"I know you've got to make a profit. I understand that perfectly well—I was in business for many years. I assumed that you'd get full catalogue, so I felt half catalogue was a fair asking price." He looked at me with cool dispassionate eyes. "Half catalogue . . . seemed a reasonable price. . . ."

"I wish I *could* get full catalogue for stamps. My check would be in your hand right now. But that's just not the case. I have to pay according to what I can charge for stamps."

"I understand. It's just so much less than I'd anticipated."

"When you stop to think about it, we're not too far apart—at least in principle. I've offered you roughly half—nearly twenty percent—of what the high end of the retail market is at the moment—about forty percent. I've shown you advertised retail prices that vary from as low as twenty-five percent to an upper limit of about forty percent.

"Some countries, such as Germany, are worth higher percentages of catalogue than others, such as Ghana. And older stamps from the 1930s, 1940s, and 1950s are generally worth a greater percentage of catalogue than stamps from the 1960s onward. The desirable material balances the not-so-desirable. Your collection's primarily never-hinged—and comprehensive—so I can stretch a bit. If it weren't as comprehensive and balanced as it is, I would offer only about fifteen percent of catalogue."

He listened, but I couldn't tell if I was making any headway. I wanted to buy the collection badly. I could only hope that the evidence I had presented would persuade him to sell. But he remained stone faced, giving no indication of what he planned to do.

"I've shown you current retail ads and auction prices. They're a matter of record. Based on the market, my offer is reasonable and along the guidelines you mentioned—selling at half retail."

"I'm sure it is," he said finally. "Still, I had hoped to get so much more. I'm not sure I want to let my stamps go for the price you've offered." His voice was firm, yet hesitant. It sounded as if he were leaning away from selling, but hadn't ruled it out.

"You could get another offer, but I don't think it would be much different from mine—the market *is* the market. When I give an offer, I always assume it will be measured against others. The last thing I'd do is make a ridiculously low offer. I can't afford to. Collections like yours don't come along every day, and when they do, a dealer's got to stretch as far as he can to buy them. I've shown you what the market is. I've made a reasonable offer. I'd very much like to buy your collection."

"I'm sure you've been straightforward, Mr. Datz. But as I said, it's so much less than I'd expected—I'm not sure I want to let it go."

I began to feel that I had not made my case. After they've finished pleading a case, do lawyers experience the same feeling as they watch the jury file silently out to deliberate? I looked at those beautiful green albums, suspecting I would leave without them.

We sat silently for a moment, each of us alone with his thoughts. Then, Chapman said, "Excuse me. I want to talk this over with my wife."

"Take your time. I'm in no hurry."

While he was gone, I absentmindedly paged through a few albums. Mylar mounts gave the stamps a glossy look, made their colors deep and rich, like those of photographs in expensive, slick magazines. *Perhaps I should have offered more,* I thought. *Perhaps I ought to offer more.* Then, I thought, *No, don't get carried away. Every time you do, you make a bad buy.* But, another voice said, *Don't let it slip between your fingers.*

After a few minutes, Mr. Chapman returned and sat down.

"I think the time has come to sell," he said. A thrill surged through me. I'd expected the worst.

"I've had many year's enjoyment from the collection, and I hate to see it go, but the time has come." He stroked one of the green Scott albums gently as if brushing off a bit of dust.

"I'm not getting any younger. At my age . . . well, things can happen, and I'd rather not burden my wife with having to dispose of it. She'd worry about whether she was getting the right price, and that wouldn't be fair to her. And the cost . . . it's so expensive to keep up with new issues these days. . . ."

I nodded silently.

"I used to pride myself on keeping it current," he said wistfully. "But I just don't have the energy any more." He looked up from the album and forced a smile, but couldn't hide the sadness in his eyes. He remained silent for a long moment, stroking the green album absentmindedly.

The thrill of making the deal gave way to a bittersweet sensation. Suddenly, I realized I was about to take something very special from someone who had devoted a lifetime to creating it. I appreciated how difficult it must be for him to say goodbye.

He looked up from the album he had been thoughtfully caressing and said, "So, best let someone else enjoy it." His face brightened. "Eighty thousand. Isn't that the figure you quoted?"

"Yes, sir."

"Fine," he said, "That'll be just fine."

While I filled out the check, he rounded up a dozen or so cardboard cartons in which to pack the albums. When I had finished, I handed him the check. He put it squarely on the corner of the green felt desk blotter and anchored it with the paperweight containing the chrome-yellow butterfly.

Then, he held the iron security gate open for me while I loaded carton after carton into my station wagon. He followed me out as I carried the last carton. I slid it into the back of the station wagon, and we shook hands.

"Thank you, Mr. Datz," he said, smiling.

"Thank *you*, Mr. Chapman," I said, returning his smile, grateful that he had decided to sell his collection to me.

I paused at the end of the curved driveway to check for oncoming traffic. I turned left into the street, driving past the Chapman residence. As I did, Edson Chapman was just pushing his front door closed behind the iron security gate.

The Chapman collection was the nicest—condition-wise—I had ever purchased. As I sat alone in the motel room in Albuquerque, paging through Billy Masterson's brother's collection, I appreciated just how few and far between the really good ones are—and how lucky you are when you're able to buy one.

Chapter 16

My next appointment in Albuquerque took me to a nicely land-scaped suburban home. A pleasant woman greeted me cordially at the front door and showed me into the study.

"Mr. Datz, how nice of you to come," the elderly gentleman said, extending his hand. He sat in a wheelchair and wore blue pajamas with white lapels and quilted slippers. A red plaid tartan covered his legs.

I took his hand. It felt like the hand of a skeleton. It was nothing more than bone covered by a thin, parchment-like layer of skin. I nearly shivered, but James Willoughby smiled warmly, and the impulse passed in an instant.

"Come, sit down," he said. "I've got some very nice stamps to show you."

Willoughby's pale, sunken, skeletal features gave him the appearance of being ancient and very fragile. It was obvious that he was in poor health, but he smiled cheerfully and his smile made me forget that.

"The collection's right here," he said, motioning to a nearby desk. "I hope you have enough light."

"It's fine," I assured him. The desk was near a north-facing window. Indirect, pure, white light, the kind artists prize so highly, shone through gauzy drapes. One couldn't have asked for more ideal viewing conditions. A dozen Scott albums stood on the desk, like green soldiers at attention, awaiting my inspection.

"That first album's Haiti. Spent a few years down there after the war. Helped them set up a plant. God-awful humidity. Not good for stamps. Go ahead, take a look."

I cracked Willoughby's first album and paged through it. It appeared fairly complete. Checking the backs of the stamps, I was disappointed to find that most were slightly discolored by rust-colored tropical foxing.

Tropical climates are hard on stamps. I recalled the real estate executive from Denver who had moved to Hawaii, later to discover every one of his pristine mint U.S. stamps stuck down to album pages. He was sick over it, and so was I when I saw it. He switched to used stamps, trading the stuck-down mint stamps—at deep discounts—for used Hawaiian stamps.

"Got hooked on Central America," Willoughby said. "Collected Dominican Republic, Guatemala, Nicaragua, Costa Rica, and El Salvador. But Haiti is the most complete. Never got interested in Mexico. Don't know why. Maybe all the watermarks. Too damn confusing."

I looked the albums over as he spoke. The Haiti was the best of the group, the others were spotty, a standoff between empty spaces and spaces with stamps.

"You could live like a king down there in those days. They used to like Americans . . . and everything was cheap. Had a big house, maids and a gardener, and they were glad to have the work. But the climate stunk—literally."

I visualized Willoughby—forty years younger and forty pounds heavier—wearing a white tropical suit and straw hat, sitting in a fan-back chair on a wide veranda sipping an ice-filled drink. A large, long-tailed, green macaw dozed on a tall T-perch behind him.

"Excuse me, would you like a cup of coffee?" Mrs. Willoughby said, entering the room, dispelling my daydream.

"Tea, if you have it," I said, "or water. I'm not much of a coffee drinker."

"You're not feeling too tired are you, Jim?" she said looking at Willoughby. He shook his head. "Jim can only be up for short periods of time," she said, as if to alert me to work expeditiously so as not to tire him too much.

"Oh, I'll be fine, Alma," he said, brushing aside her comment. "It's not often I get a stamp visitor. Who knows when I'll get another?"

"Okay," she said gently, "but don't overdo it." Then, she left the room.

"Where was I?" he said.

"Talking about Haiti."

"Oh, yeah. It was great in those days, before all the turmoil, but I don't think I'd want to live there now," he said, shaking his head. "The politics of the region are crazy—revolutions, assassinations, bombings. You never know what's going to happen next. You can't imagine conditions down there unless you've been there."

I listened, paging through albums.

"Animales con nombres," he said, "Animals with names—that's what they call the peasants in that part of the world. They're dirt-poor. I couldn't live like that, but they've been doing it for centuries.

"I had a good stamp collecting friend in Guatemala. He was always concerned about the political instability. Especially after the Arbenz affair in 1954. My friend was a pragmatist. 'You've got the very, very rich, the very, very poor, and the military,' he used to say. 'Go about your business, don't make any enemies, and pray for stability.' That's how he summed up his philosophy of life in Guatemala.

"And nowadays, they don't like Americans. What's going on in the world, anyway?"

I shrugged and said, "I once bought the entire stock of a Nicaraguan stamp dealer who had fled the country after the Sandinistas ousted Somoza. The stamps had been stripped out of stockbooks and condensed into glassines to save weight. The dealer had lost nearly everything in the revolution—his home, furniture, automobiles, the bulk of his clothes, bank accounts, everything that couldn't physically be taken out of the country. He managed to escape with his stamps, some jewelry and silver, and little else.

"His stock was remarkable—tens of thousands of stamps, including a wealth of esoteric material. The airmail issues of 1937 and 1938 were plentiful in all kinds of combinations—inverted centers, changed colors, imperfs, double centers—just about anything imaginable. Scott notes these varieties as private fabrications, but the quality was the same as the issued stamps.

"I'm no authority on Nicaraguan stamps, but it appeared that those issues had been printed locally—probably at a newspaper print shop. And the printer—who may have been a collector or had a friend who was—decided to have a little fun. He created every possible kind of error. The stock contained loads of un-catalogued, specialist material. And tens of thousands of used stamps, all in little bundles neatly packed like bricks into several large cardboard cartons, the whole works heavy with the fragrance of tropical mildew.

"I offered the accumulation intact to a collector I thought might be interested in owning the world's largest, most comprehensive stock of Nicaragua. I can't reveal the actual price, but just for the sake of the story, I'll use a figure of $10,000. The collector sounded interested, but passed.

"So, I offered it to a dealer in Florida who I knew had an interest in Central American stamps. He bought it over the phone, sight unseen, based on my description. No sooner had I packed and shipped it, than the collector called back saying he'd changed his mind and wanted it.

"He was very disappointed when I told him it was gone and asked if there was any possibility of getting it back. I agreed to find out, but told him not to get his hopes up.

"I called the Florida dealer and asked if he'd sell the whole works back to me. I offered him a profit, naturally. He said he'd taken out what he wanted—noting that he hadn't stripped it too badly—and would be happy to sell it back to me for what he had paid for it. His profit would be in the items he kept. 'Great,' I said, 'ship it back.'

"I told the collector that he could have the lot, minus the few items the Florida dealer had kept, for the original asking price plus ten percent. The ten percent compensated me for my trouble in bouncing it around. The collector didn't hesitate. I think he realized that comprehensive stocks, such as this one, don't come on the market every day. After he received the lot, he called to tell me how much he liked it. He still has it to this day," I said.

"Boy, aren't stamps great?" Willoughby said, his ancient face animated and happy. I was glad to see him enjoying himself.

Mrs. Willoughby returned with a cup of tea for me and something in a tumbler for Willoughby. She adjusted his plaid tartan, which had begun to slip.

"Oh, don't fuss over me, Alma," he objected weakly.

"You've got to stay warm," she said, "And I don't want you to get too tired."

"I'll be fine," he insisted.

"Okay," Mrs. Willoughby said, "but let me know if you get tired."

"I will, Alma," he said. "I will."

I realized I should proceed more quickly. Willoughby entertained me with anecdotes about his life in Haiti while I worked. It didn't take long to finish.

When I had closed the last album, he spoke, seriously and matter-of-factly. "I have terminal cancer," he said.

I had suspected as much, judging from his appearance. Still, hearing him say it saddened me.

"In fact, I don't have long—a few weeks, if I'm lucky. I've enjoyed the stamps immensely, but need to make arrangements to dispose of them. Don't want to leave any unfinished business for Alma." He spoke unemotionally.

I nodded and felt uncomfortable, the feeling you get when you think there's something you ought to say or do—but know there isn't.

"So, that brings us to the point, Mr. Datz. Are you interested in buying the collection?"

"How much do you want for it?"

"Ten thousand dollars."

"I don't think I'm your man, Mr. Willoughby," I said, taken aback by the figure. "Your asking price is about double what I could get for it."

He looked at me for a moment and sighed. "What can you offer?"

"I really don't think it would do any good to make an offer. It would be substantially less what you're asking."

"Go ahead. You won't offend me."

I had heard that before and knew that, regardless of what people said, they usually were offended by a realistic offer. As I looked at Jim Willoughby, thin as a concentration camp inmate. I didn't want to tell him what his collection was really worth and destroy one of his few remaining expectations. I hesitated.

"Don't be bashful, Mr. Datz," he said.

I drew a deep breath and said, "My offer would be in the two to three thousand dollar range. I'm sorry it's not more, but that's the market."

Willoughby looked very disappointed. His cheerfulness vanished. With nothing to mask the ravages of cancer, he suddenly looked old and very tired. It was as if he'd withered before my eyes.

"I'll have to think about it, Mr. Datz," he said softly, as if his strength, too, had faded with his smile. "Can you call me tomorrow morning? I'll give you an answer then."

"I'd be glad to," I said, rising, suddenly uncomfortable and anxious not to tire him further.

Mrs. Willoughby showed me out. "Call any time after eight," she said. "We're usually up pretty early."

I thanked her and left.

The rest of the day proved unrewarding. I spent a couple hours looking over a modern plate block and mint sheet accumulation. The stamps were nothing more than discount postage.

"But stamps are supposed to be a good investment!" the owner protested. I had heard that frustrated reaction too many times. I was in no mood for lengthy explanations about the folly of hoarding modern sheets, how they were a glut on the market. I thanked him and left.

The next collection consisted of a couple boxes of envelope clippings. I was in and out in 15 minutes, fourteen of which were spent on pleasantries.

When I'd finished, I stopped for a cheeseburger and fries, then returned to the motel. I spent the evening looking over the

Masterson collection again, hoping to find at least a few stamps that hadn't been abused but didn't have any luck.

I called Willoughby promptly at eight the next morning.

"I've decided to keep the stamps," Willoughby said. "But I'd like you to stop by. I've got something for you."

I was disappointed and wished that he had not asked me to come over. Much as I enjoyed chatting with Willoughby, I didn't want to delay my departure for Denver any longer than necessary. Nevertheless, I went.

"Go ahead. Take a look," he said, pointing to a large box next to the desk.

The box brimmed with foreign revenue stamps—all off paper, all jumbled up. It must have weighed ten pounds. I rummaged through it. I had no idea what it might be worth, no idea where to find out.

"I've put you to a lot of trouble," he said, "What with making the trip down here and all. Your offer for the collection is probably fair, but it's much less than I'd hoped for. Two or three thousand dollars isn't going to change Alma's life. I've decided to pass it on to my son-in-law. He's expressed an interest in it, and perhaps someday it'll be worth more. In the meantime, I want you to have this for your trouble. It's yours. Go ahead and take it. And thanks again for your time and trouble."

"It was no trouble at all," I said, disappointed at not getting the collection, thinking how little I had to show for the trip, then realizing how fortunate I was. The man seated in front of me would almost certainly not live to see the new year.

"Have a good trip back," Willoughby said, extending his hand.

I shook it and, again, felt the ancient bones beneath his fragile skin.

"Thanks," I said.

Mrs. Willoughby showed me out.

It was just after nine in the morning when I turned onto Interstate 25 and began the long trip north. Snow began to fall as I crossed the border into Colorado. By the time I reached Colorado Springs, the weather had badly deteriorated; I was in the middle of the worst snow storm I've ever driven through. Just north of Colorado Springs, cars, like wounded beasts, littered the ice-covered approach to Monument Hill, one of the most treacherous stretches of Interstate 25 in bad weather. The road hadn't been sanded yet and was slick as wet glass. Cars that slowed too much found it impossible to regain forward momentum. They spun their wheels in a vain attempt to move forward, but only succeeded in sliding onto the shoulder, then into the ditch at the side of the road. There they struggled helplessly, like insects trying to escape from a pitcher plant.

I made it to the crest of the hill—just barely. I crawled along at less than thirty miles an hour. Heavy, wet spring snow came down so furiously that I could only see a few feet ahead in the deepening twilight. The sticky snow clogged my wipers, but I didn't dare stop for fear of getting stuck or being hit from behind. I banged on the wipers with the yard-long handle of a snow scraper and managed to keep them just clear enough to navigate. The highway had not yet been plowed, and at times I wasn't sure if I was even on the road. I crept along, increasingly worried that I wasn't going to make it to Denver.

South of Castle Rock, a car pulled onto the highway ahead of me from an entrance ramp. It was a state trooper. I was able keep up with him, grateful for his tire tracks to guide me in the blinding storm. I felt safer, confident that if I went off the road, help was near at hand. Then, I realized that if I needed help, I could only honk, which he probably wouldn't hear in snow as dense as attic insulation, or blink my lights, which he probably wouldn't see. If I went off the road, he wouldn't be able to help me. I fought to keep him in sight and prayed that he wouldn't speed up. I crawled along behind him for nearly an hour, until at last I could see the glow of Denver's lights ahead.

Sue was waiting when I pulled into the garage.

"I was worried," she said. "I didn't think you'd make it."

"Neither did I," I said climbing out of the car. My fingers ached from gripping the steering wheel too tightly for so long. "Worst drive I've ever made."

"Did you buy anything?"

"Yeah, a candidate for world's worst collection. The other leads didn't amount to much, except one, which the man decided to keep. He did give me a box of foreign revenues, though, but who knows what they're worth? The expense of the trip, and then the storm. Sometimes I wonder if it's worth it . . ."

"C'mon in. I've got a pot of hot soup on, and I'll make you a sandwich. Things will look brighter tomorrow."

Postscript. I priced Masterson's brother's collection at approximately four percent of catalogue. I marked the cover of each album with the catalogue value and sale price, such as "$1,500 Catalogue, Special $60!" I hauled the albums from show to show, but the condition was so terrible that one look frightened potential buyers away despite the enormous discount from catalogue. Only a few albums sold. Eventually, I put the remainder in auction as one bulk lot. When the dust settled, I'd made a profit of less than $100 on the Masterson collection.

Chapter 17

When there's a foot of snow on the ground in Denver and the temperature sinks to ten below zero, it's great to escape to warm places such as California or Florida. I had swaying palms, gentle sea breezes, and a successful buying trip in mind when I flew to Los Angeles in January 1984. I'd made appointments to view three collections and hoped I could buy them all.

The first man had raved about his collection on the telephone. It was one of those *I inherited it, but have no idea what it's worth* deals—short on specifics, long on possibilities.

"My uncle kept his stamps in a safe deposit box," the caller had said. "Some envelopes are marked *rare* or *scarce*."

So, when the man appeared at my hotel door in Los Angeles, I expected to see valuable stamps. He smiled, breezed into the room as though he owned it, and took a seat at the small table near the window. He was in his late twenties. His smile, speech, and energetic manner reminded me of a small waggy-tailed dog, the kind that won't stop jumping up and pestering you. After enthusiastically retelling the history of the stamps, he opened his cordovan-colored attaché case and removed two cigar boxes. As soon as I saw them, I knew I had wasted my time. Nevertheless, I looked through them.

"You're stamps are worth about twenty bucks," I said, wondering why anyone would keep junk stamps in a safe deposit box. "At least, that's what you can expect to be offered if you shop them around."

The news triggered a barrage of questions: "How can you be so sure? You barely looked at them. What about the notes on the glassines?"

"I'm not making an offer," I said. "I'm just telling you what to expect if you visit other dealers. If your stamps were desirable, I'd try to negotiate a deal, but they're not. I can't use them." He harumphed, replaced the boxes in his expensive-looking attaché case, and departed as hastily as he had entered.

My next appointment took me to Anaheim. After nearly an hour of driving, missing freeway exits, and struggling with a map, I found the address. I parked my rented station wagon—being an optimist, I had rented a station wagon so I would have plenty of room for all the stamps I hoped to buy—and rang the doorbell. A heavy-set, middle-aged woman in a loose flowery muumuu greeted me at the door. She ushered me into the kitchen, her brightly-colored, billowing muumuu fluttering in her wake, thong sandals slapping against the bottoms of her feet. Several albums were stacked on the kitchen table. A dilapidated cardboard carton sat on the floor next to the table.

"Would you like a guava cooler?" she asked. "It's fresh." Containers of wheat germ, honey, and a variety of health foods crowded the counter. A large, complex-looking blender occupied the center of the counter, like the queen on a chessboard.

"No, thanks," I said. "But I could use a glass of water."

She reached into the refrigerator, filled a tumbler from a gallon jug. "Distilled," she said, handing me the glass. "I don't trust tap water." I smiled and took a sip. She settled into a chair on the opposite side of the table.

"I've had these stamps for years. My father gave them to me, but I never really got interested in keeping the collection up."

I flipped through a red Scott Indian Chief album and several three-ring binders containing foreign stamps. The stamps were common. The carton contained tongs, magnifier, hinges, blank pages, and a tantalizing chunk of part sheets and blocks—two-cent reds and stamps from the 1930s, by the look of it. The chunk was about half an inch thick and solidly stuck together. I tried bending it to see if it would pop apart, but it was hard and unyielding.

Only soaking would separate the stamps. The albums smelled moldy, and the pages were slightly warped.

"Looks like the collection got wet," I said.

"The garage leaked. I didn't realize the stamps were wet until it was too late." She didn't seem concerned or even aware that moisture had greatly reduced the value of her stamps.

"If they hadn't gotten wet, I could offer a lot more, but the way it is, they're worth about seventy-five dollars," I said.

"What about those stamps?" the woman asked, pointing to the brick-like chunk.

"Looks like common two-cent reds," I said. "They've got to be soaked apart, and, without gum, they'll have little philatelic value. They're just postage. I'm just guessing, but I'd say face value is around twenty dollars—at least, that's how I figured it. Keep it if you like," I said, hefting the brick in my hand as I waited for her to make up her mind.

"Oh, well, go ahead and take it," she said.

I loaded the dilapidated box into my station wagon and pulled out, hoping I wouldn't get lost on the way to my next appointment.

The third collection belonged to a veterinarian. He'd told me on the phone that it catalogued nearly $100,000. I found his clinic without a problem. A receptionist ushered me into an examining room where about twenty Minkus international albums stood arranged on a counter next to swabs, sterile cotton, bandages, and other medical supplies.

I'd been there only a couple of minutes when the veterinarian entered the room and introduced himself. "The collection belonged to a friend who died recently," he said. "I bought it from the estate. It contains a fair number of valuable stamps, according to the inventory." He retrieved a thick file folder from the end of the row of albums, opened it, handed it to me, and said, "Everything's itemized."

I immediately noticed that the inventory followed an interesting pattern. The most expensive stamps were clustered at the beginning of each section.

"I felt I was doing the estate a favor by buying it, rather than letting some local dealer get it for next to nothing," he said, as I looked over the inventory.

I didn't care for his comment. I took it to mean that he regarded local dealers, in specific, and all dealers, in general, as disreputable.

"The collection catalogues ninety-seven-some thousand dollars," he said. "It's all there in the inventory."

"Did you make the inventory?"

"No, the owner did."

"Do you know what year catalogue he used?"

"Eighty or eighty-one, I think. The value's probably higher by now."

"No. Catalogue values are down," I said.

"Oh?" he said, raising his eyebrows. "I thought stamps rose in value every year."

"Not necessarily. The recession of 1981 took the wind out of their sails. What kind of money are you looking for?"

"I don't really know," he said, "I was hoping you'd make an offer."

I knew from experience that sellers always have a figure in mind, but decided not to press him. "I'll need a few minutes to look it over," I said.

"Go ahead, take your time. I've got some patients to attend to. Let me know when you're finished." And with that he whisked off, leaving me alone in the white-walled examining room.

I worked, listening to barks, whines, and other animal sounds, wondering if he treated exotic jungle animals. When I had finished, I ventured into the hallway, hoping I wouldn't encounter a lion or some other unusual beast.

"I'm ready whenever the doctor is," I told the receptionist.

"I'll let him know, but it'll be a few minutes. He's got a python with a problem," she said, making it sound routine. I went back to the examining room and waited.

"Nice collection, isn't it?" the veterinarian said ten minutes later, swinging the door open. "So, what did you come up with?"

"Well, you've got lots of stamps, but most of the catalogue value is in used nineteenth-century issues, and condition is a problem."

The vet frowned.

"The only used nineteenth-century stamps worth anywhere near catalogue value are premium copies—stamps free of defects and in top condition. The kind that walk on water. The vast majority of nineteenth-century stamps are faulty, which is why they trade at such great discounts from catalogue."

"So, what are you getting at?" he snapped.

"I'm just explaining the facts of life—marketwise—so you'll understand what I've based my offer on."

"And what is your offer?" he said, sounding confrontational. I sensed we weren't going to make a deal, and I couldn't see any point in getting into an argument.

"Because the bulk of the catalogue value is in early faulty material, my offer would be less than ten percent of catalogue."

"If I had wanted to give it away, I'd have let the local yokels buy it," he snarled.

"How much did you expect to get?"

"Not ten percent of catalogue."

"How much then?"

"That's irrelevant. You don't want to pay anywhere near what it's worth, so what's the point in discussing it?"

"Look, I've taken the trouble to come out here. I've told you what I'd pay. I've been straightforward with you—the least you can do is tell me how much you wanted. All I'm hearing are insinuations that I'm not paying enough. Name your figure . . . unless you're embarrassed to."

"Forty-five thousand," he said sharply.

"It's not worth forty-five thousand. Here let me show you." I was about to retrieve some retail ads and auction realizations to illustrate my point.

But the veterinarian ignored me, rearranged the albums on the counter, tucked the inventory back where it had been.

"The collection's not for sale," he said brusquely. "Our business is concluded. I'm a busy man, got patients waiting. If you were serious about buying the collection, I'd talk further. But you're not, so there's no use wasting time." He swung the door open and extended his arm, indicating I should leave. I hastened to put my things back into my attaché case, while he stood impatiently at the door.

I had intended to show him results from recent New York auctions. They're good guides to market value. Collections similar to his had been selling at auction for between five and ten percent of catalogue at the time, and the heavier the concentration of nineteenth-century material, the closer to the five percent mark. One example, a collection of early France cataloguing $52,500 had sold for $2,500—five percent of catalogue. I felt like telling him off but thought better of it. The deal was dead, and an exchange of words would not bring it back to life, so I left.

When I had had a chance to think about it, I concluded that he'd bought the collection from the estate for more than ten percent, probably around 20-25 percent, hoping to sell it for 40 percent. Unfortunately, he had paid too much. I didn't believe for a minute his claim about wanting to help the estate by paying more than the local dealers. Although, the way it worked out, he had helped the estate. He'd paid considerably more than any dealer would have. I attributed his ill temper to the fact that it was beginning to dawn on him that his scheme had backfired.

I returned to Denver disappointed that the only thing I had to show for my trouble was a small moldy collection. A few days later, I soaked the brick of two-cent reds in a tub. Toward the end, I swirled the water to make sure all the stamps had soaked free. In the flurry of red commemoratives, I noticed a flash of green and brown. Scarcely believing my eyes, I fished out a single copy each of the 65-cent and $1.30 Zeppelin stamps. Even without gum, they were worth several hundred dollars. That stroke of luck reduced the financial pain of the trip and reinforced something I had come to understand about buying trips: there's often a wild card in the deck.

Chapter 18

In August 1990, Rafael Griswold called me again to discuss the sale of his sizable collection of airmail covers. The collection had been on the market for several years, the asking price as high as $150,000, a completely unrealistic figure.

"Listen," Griswold said, "I've been thinking over what you said about the collection being priced too high, and I'm willing to take fifty thousand. That's a firm figure—not a penny more, not a penny less."

I got the impression that Griswold thought I ought to jump at his offer, that his reducing the price to $50,000 was a great concession. We had discussed the collection for years. But he had an extravagantly inflated notion of its value. I had never made an offer. It wouldn't have done any good; we were too far apart. Instead, I had alluded to a price range I thought realistic, thinking that if he sounded interested, I'd talk concrete figures. Unfortunately, he was incapable of focusing on anything but his own unrealistic estimate of the retail value of the covers. He based his asking price on a discount from that inflated retail level.

I might have jumped at a price of $50,000 a few years earlier, but not now. In August 1990, Iraq had just invaded Kuwait, the price of oil was skyrocketing, financial markets had jitters, and recession was in the wind. The mood was anything but optimistic.

A few years earlier, I had tried to sell some of Griswold's covers on a commission basis. Even that had been a mistake. The retail prices he had insisted on were too high, and there were no takers. Eventually, I stopped trying and returned them to him.

I had never given him reason to believe I'd pay $50,000 for his covers. It was just another of his assumptions. Since, however, he was in a selling mood, I put pencil to paper as we spoke and tried to calculate a reasonable figure. I arrived at $25,000—half what he wanted.

As usual, Griswold did most of the talking. He wasn't a good listener. His ideas tended to be set in concrete, and the opinions of others had about as much effect on him as a breeze on a skyscraper.

"How did you arrive at fifty thousand?" I asked, when at last I could get a word in edgewise.

"Simple. You got a thousand covers at fifty bucks a pop. Some are worth a hundred bucks, two hundred bucks, even four or five hundred bucks."

"True, but they're in the small minority. You've also got hundreds of covers that aren't worth ten dollars retail."

"You're underestimating the good stuff," he insisted, itemizing a few key items.

"I don't think so. Besides, the market's kind of funny right now. No one knows what's going to happen in Iraq or how this recession's going to turn out. The stamp market could get real soft, real fast."

"And the world could end tomorrow," he said sarcastically, reminding me how impossible it was to reason with him.

"Nevertheless, I don't think the collection's worth fifty thousand right now."

"Okay, what are you willing to pay?"

"Twenty-five thousand."

"Oh, come on, I'm not playing give-away!"

"We've been talking about your collection for years. Every six months you call me, and we talk some more, but we never get anywhere. You're just not realistic about the value of your covers. If you were, you'd have sold them by now—if not to me, then to someone else. I tried to sell some at *your* prices—remember—and we had no luck. Why? Because they were priced too high! We're just not getting anywhere, so why bother?"

"Look, I am serious about selling the covers," he said calmly, the sarcasm gone from his voice. "I don't think fifty thousand is excessive."

"Well, that's your opinion. You know mine. I'm interested at twenty-five thousand."

"Would you go forty thousand?"

"No. Sorry."

"Thirty-five thousand?" he said in an uncharacteristically pleasant tone.

"Twenty-five thousand—tops."

"Thirty-five thousand isn't unreasonable. I've come down fifteen thousand. You should be willing to give a little."

"If I thought we were playing a game, I'd have started at fifteen thousand and settled at twenty-five. Maybe I should have done that, but I didn't, so I'm stuck at twenty-five with no room to maneuver."

"You're squeezing me real hard. Asking for a big concession—you ought to help out. How about thirty thousand?" Griswold was persistent if nothing else. "You can stretch five thousand. That's only fair."

"I'm willing to pay twenty-five thousand cash right now. At thirty thousand, I'll have to pass." I didn't feel like stretching. I had wasted too many hours over the years haggling with Griswold. I'd reached the end of my patience. I didn't care if I bought the covers or not.

I heard a long loud sigh, as if I'd done something highly unsportsmanlike. "Okay, twenty-five thousand."

I couldn't believe my ears. I felt mildly exhilarated for the briefest moment at having made a deal that had dangled for years.

"When can we close?" Griswold asked.

"Right away. Ship the covers, and I'll mail you a check."

"No, I want cash. We'll have to close the deal in person."

"I'm not flying to New York with twenty-five thousand in cash."

"Maybe we could meet somewhere in between?"

"That's not the point. It's too risky to carry that much cash around."

"Well, you could bring a cashier's check to New York and cash it here."

"Look, if you don't trust me, we shouldn't be doing business. I can give you bank references if you like."

"Oh, it's not that. Cash has its own magic, if you get my drift."

"Magic?"

"You know, it's invisible . . . as in not seen by the IRS."

"Oh, I see. Well, you could always come to Denver." I didn't mind paying cash if that's what a man wanted. What he did with it was his affair. My attorney, who sounded as if he had been born and bred in West Texas, once told me, "Hell, son, cash is legal tender. That's why it was invented. What a man does with the money after you give it to him is between him and his conscience. Whether another man pays his taxes or not is no concern of yours. Just get a bill of sale."

"I really don't have the time to fly to Denver," Griswold said.

I was annoyed. There was no satisfying the man. Instead of getting simpler, the deal was getting more complicated.

"Maybe we ought to forget the whole thing," I said.

"How about I pay your way to New York? I'll deduct the price of your ticket from the twenty-five thousand."

I should have said no. Instead, I began thinking about all the things I could do on a free trip to New York.

"I don't know," I said, weakening, "There's the cost of cabs, hotel, meals. It's still expensive."

"Okay, I'll pick them up, too."

Griswold was being awfully agreeable after the fuss he'd made over the asking price. Suddenly, I felt claustrophobic. I needed breathing space.

"Let me check the airlines. I'll get back to you tomorrow," I said, tabling negotiations.

"Fine, do that. Call me as soon as you've made arrangements."

That night, I went to sleep feeling vaguely uneasy. I woke up sometime after midnight and couldn't get back to sleep. A thought kept running through my head: *I shouldn't have bought the covers.* It had nothing to do with the trip to New York, which was a separate annoying issue, but hinged on the covers themselves. The more I thought about it, the more certain I was that even at

$25,000, I'd made a poor decision. I kept thinking about the economy and the threat of war. *Bad move,* I told myself, *very bad move!*

As I lay there in the cold embrace of buyer's remorse, I struggled to think of a way out of the deal, but couldn't find an honorable path. I'd said I would buy the covers, and I would have to honor my word. I resigned myself to that and finally went back to sleep about four o'clock.

I called my travel agent the next morning. Between the air fare, hotel, and incidentals, the cost of the trip would amount to nearly $1,000. I decided not to dwell on my unwise purchase. Instead, I concentrated on strategies to market the covers, to get as much money back as quickly as I could. I would be lucky to recoup $10,000 quickly, and it might take a year or two to get the other $15,000 back, let alone turn a profit. I should have considered that before I had made the deal. The more I thought about it, the more I realized I'd made a mistake.

About noon, the phone rang.

"How are you today?" Griswold began, the boisterous assertiveness absent from his voice. "About our deal . . ."

Now what? I thought. *It's a dumb deal to begin with, the trip adds insult to injury, now what does he want?* I had had enough. I wanted no further complications.

"I was talking it over with my wife last night . . ."

Why was he hemming and hawing?

"Anyway, we decided we've got to get fifty thousand. Twenty-five just won't do. She was real mad at me for saying I'd take twenty-five. She's got her heart set on fifty thousand, not a penny more, not a penny less." He sounded embarrassed.

He had made an offer, I had accepted. Legally, we had a contract, albeit an oral one. I knew that much from business law. Now, Griswold was trying to back out. After all the phone calls, after all the hours of putting up with his abrasive negotiating style, I wanted to shout, *Look, you jerk! We had a deal, and I'm holding you to it. You think you can make a deal one day and weasel out of it the next? No way! You made a deal, and, by God, you're going to honor it!* If I had really wanted the deal, I would have said those things—and angrily! But I didn't want the deal. Griswold had just answered my prayers. He'd given me a way out.

"Well, I'll have to pass," I said, relieved the moment the words crossed my lips.

The line remained silent for a long moment. Then, I heard the muffled sound of Griswold's voice. He had covered the receiver with his palm and was giving his wife the news.

"The fifty thousand is not negotiable," he said, coming back on the line, as if confident that—when faced with that immutable fact— I would cave in and pay his price. However, as far as I was concerned negotiations were finished.

"Like I said, I'll have to pass."

"Well, if you change your mind, let me know. Just remember the price is fifty thousand, not a penny more, not a penny less."

Was it my imagination or did his tone imply that sooner or later I would come to my senses and meet his price?

"I'm curious," I said, "Yesterday, you were ready to sell for twenty-five thousand. Today, it's fifty thousand. Why the flip-flop?"

"Sorry," he said, lowering his voice to a whisper, "my wife insists on fifty thousand."

"Does your wife collect? I mean, how did she arrive at fifty thousand?"

"My fault, I guess . . ." he paused, embarrassed by the admission. "She doesn't know anything about stamps. I've been telling her about how much we'd get for the covers. She's got her heart set on a trip and a new car, and she figures it's going to take at least fifty thousand to cover everything she's got planned."

I chuckled silently. The wife smells money, and she's going for the throat. Griswold had backed himself into a corner, but it was his own fault. Unfortunately, now they weren't going to get anything—not even the twenty-five thousand they had yesterday.

About three months later, Griswold called back.

"About the deal," he began, "I could give a little on the price, if it would help."

By that time, I had no desire to do business with Griswold at all. I don't consider myself superstitious, but I sensed that no matter how good a deal I thought I'd made, a mousetrap lay hidden, waiting to spring shut the moment I committed myself.

"Thanks, but I'm really not interested in the covers anymore."

"I thought you were a buyer at twenty-five thousand?"

"I was, but the funny thing is, after we made our deal in August, I had second thoughts. On reflection, I realized that even at twenty-five thousand, it would be months, maybe even years, before I'd recoup my original investment—and all in a very nervous market. You changed your mind, I changed mine. We were both happy."

"Well, if you change your mind—"

"I'll call you," I said, finishing the sentence for him, but knowing I never would.

"Okay," he said, "Let me know when you're ready to deal." He hung up.

I set the receiver back on its cradle, glad Griswold was unappreciative of the wisdom of the old saying: *A bird in the hand is worth two in the bush.*

Chapter 19

"I know we got us a real valuable collection here," Les Slocum said on the phone.

I asked him to describe it to me, but he couldn't seem to provide me the specifics I needed to decide whether or not to drive to Walden. All he could tell me was that the collection had belonged to his wife's grandfather, occupied a metal file cabinet and numerous boxes, and that it was valuable. About that, he was adamant. Dealers, however, know better than to pay attention to the opinions of non-collectors when it comes to value; most are unrealistic on the high side. When you've been on enough wild goose chases, you're reluctant to travel based on vague information.

While we spoke, I pulled a road atlas off the shelf to refresh my memory about Walden's location. The name Walden makes you think of rustic Walden Pond in Concord, Massachusetts, where Henry David Thoreau wrote essays on essential living. Slocum, however, lived in Walden, Colorado. I'd never been there, but I conjured visions of any idyllic town nestled high in the Colorado Rockies. According to the road atlas, Walden was located about a hundred miles northwest of Loveland. More than half the distance appeared to be mountain driving. Although it was April, stretches of road at higher elevations could still be snowpacked.

"Could you bring it to Loveland?" I asked.

"Too bulky, wouldn't fit in our Toyota."

"Can't you give me some idea of the better stamps?"

"There's everything you could think of. Stamps with cats and dogs and butterflies. Books and books full. We got boxes of stamps up here."

It sounded like a massive jumble of cancelled-to-order packet material—nothing worth driving a hundred miles through the mountains to see.

"Was he a serious collector? Does the collection have any key items such as Zeppelins?"

Pause. I could hear in the background, "Man wants to know if the collection's got any key items . . . that's what I told him . . . I don't know why all the questions . . ."

Then, back to me, "Look, we got a ton of stamps up here. I figured someone in the stamp business would be real anxious to have a shot at them. If you're not interested . . ."

"I'm always interested in buying collections. If you could bring it to Loveland, I'd be happy to look at it. It's just that a trip to Walden shoots a whole day, so I'm trying to find out if it's worthwhile before making a trip."

"We got boxes and boxes full of stamps. And that file cabinet. There's loads of stamps in them little wax paper envelopes. The man was a real hoarder. You ain't gonna be disappointed."

I had heard that before and invariably had been disappointed. However, it *was* April, and the sun shone brightly outside my window. *Why not?* I said to myself. *I could use a day out of the office.* Besides, having read *Walden* years before in college, I was curious to see what a place named Walden looked like, even if it wasn't the one in Massachusetts.

"Okay, I'll come," I said. "How about Thursday around ten? If I leave early, I think I can be there by ten."

"That would be great."

"I know how to get to Walden, but I'll need directions to your house."

"The house is kinda hard to find unless you're familiar with the town. Why don't you meet us at Milly's—it's a coffee shop right on the main drag. You can't miss it. Then you can follow us over to the house."

"All right. Give me your phone number in case something comes up and I can't make it." I was thinking of the spring snow storms that can strike without warning and bury the high country under a foot or two of snow.

"We don't have a phone," Slocum said.

Oh, brother! I thought.

"You can call my wife's sister at Milly's if something comes up, and she'll get word to us." He gave me the phone number.

Why am I wasting my time? I thought.

"You ain't gonna be disappointed."

"Okay, see you Thursday morning," I said, suddenly sure I'd made a mistake by agreeing to go.

The scenic drive to Walden cuts through Roosevelt National Forest. The day was brilliant, as if etched in crystal. The weather was so flawless and the scenery so magnificent that I decided the drive would be worth it even if the collection turned out to be nothing. On a weekday in spring, there's little traffic. I saw less than a dozen cars coming or going once I got into the mountains. The highway had been cleared and was mostly dry, except a few north-facing spots in the perpetual shadow of surrounding peaks. The road to Walden crests at Cameron Pass, located more than 10,000 feet above sea level, then descends on the west side of the Medicine Bow range.

Walden, population 947, lies in a high mountain valley about 30 miles wide. The valley is open, wind-swept country, barren except for occasional herds of cattle that wander the rangeland grazing on thin grass. Walden wasn't what I expected. It's a bare-bones town, with its sheepskin collar turned up against the relentless wind that blows in from Wyoming. Walden's main drag is short and to the point. The businesses serve ranchers and farmers. There are no boutiques, no style shops, no fast-food restaurants. Milly's was right in the middle of town and popular, judging by the number of mud-spattered pickup trucks parked in front of it.

I walked in and scanned the dozen or so tables. Milly's wasn't a quiche and de-caf kind of place. Weathered rancher faces looked up at me, no doubt wondering who the stranger in the pin-striped suit was. A large, bushy-bearded man wearing a dark wooly coat—he reminded me of a mountain man—rose from a rear table and, smiling, asked "You the stamp guy?"

"Yes," I said, "And you're Les Slocum?"

"That's right," he said, shaking my hand. He had a grip like a bear trap. "This here's my wife, Cheri." The bright-faced, red-haired woman seated at the table said softly, "Nice to meet you."

"Bring us another cup of coffee," Slocum called to the waitress behind the lunch counter, his voice so deep and resonant he didn't need to raise it to make himself heard. I'm not a coffee drinker, so I called to the waitress to make it tea. Again, the assembled Marlboro men, sipping their black coffees from white ceramic mugs, looked up in unison. I smiled and slipped into a chair.

The waitress served my tea, which I sipped sparingly, and I chatted with the Slocums for a few minutes. Then, I mentioned that it might be a good idea if I got started on the collection so I would have plenty of time. I wanted to wrap it up and get back to Loveland at a decent hour.

"You betcha," Slocum said. He tipped his cup back draining the last of his coffee, rose, tossed a dollar on the table, and we walked out.

I followed Slocum's unwashed yellow Toyota. Walden is a small town. I wouldn't have had any trouble finding his house, so I wondered why he hadn't given me directions instead of wanting to meet at Milly's. Perhaps he thought I wasn't smart enough to find my way.

It took only a couple of minutes to reach the Slocum's house, a tiny, old, gray, frame structure that had a patched-together look. Inside, the curtains were drawn, making it feel even smaller than it was. I felt certain I had wasted a trip. I wanted to look at the stamps and be on my way. Slocum invited me to have a seat on the sofa while he fetched a cardboard carton.

"Here's the cats and dogs," he said, pulling out a three-ring binder, handing it to me. "Ain't they pretty?" he asked as I flipped through pages of animal topicals, including butterflies, fish, and reptiles. It was inexpensive packet material. Cheri started to raise one of the shades, but Slocum cautioned, "Don't put those up too high. You know how damn nosey the neighbors are." She lifted them just enough to brighten the room.

It took less than five minutes to inspect the carton full of binders. The whole works didn't amount to $100. While I worked, Slocum brought in several more cartons and a small metal filing cabinet, the size used to store four-by-six cards.

The second carton surprised me. It contained an Israel collection, including all the key sets with tabs. Another album contained U.S. commemorative plate blocks back to the Pilgrim issue, all in mounts, most never-hinged, plus the Presidential and Liberty series complete. Cheri's grandfather had stuffed numerous mint duplicates into a large Elbe stockbook. It included dozens of nearly every commemorative back to the World War I victory issue; scattered Kansas-Nebraska issues; two 1922 series $5 Americas; extra Presidential and Liberty high-values; dozens of Presidential line pairs, including the 10-cent value; and many more.

A mint sheet file contained half a dozen White Plains sheets, plus sheets and part sheets of numerous airmail issues. I counted two sets of transport planes, six 80-cent Diamond Head sheets, and many others. Then, I hit a run of commemorative mint sheet files. The face value alone amounted to $3,000.

The metal filing cabinet was jammed with new issues still in glassines: United Nations, Ghana, Israel, Germany, Switzerland, and others. I plodded along, surprised by the abundance and quality of material, hoping my calculator's batteries would hold up. After the first disappointing box, everything had been wonderful.

At lunch time, Cheri served turkey sandwiches with a big kosher dill and potato chips. Les finished his sandwich in three or four bites, the pickle in two crunches. Cheri followed the sandwiches with freshly made blueberry tarts whose crust, like butter on an August day, melted in my mouth.

After lunch, I came across a mint U.S. collection, which, although hinged, contained a handsome run of Washington-Franklins, complete Columbians and Trans-Mississippis (the dollar values were used). The collection seemed to go on and on.

"Why didn't you mention this stuff on the phone?" I asked.

"I did. I told you there was tons of stuff."

"But you didn't mention the valuable stamps."

"Sure, I did. I told you there was lots of valuable stamps."

"You mentioned dogs and cats—"

"Look, I don't know one stamp from another. I know what's pretty, so that's what I told you about."

"But the real value is in the other stamps."

"Well, they didn't look too good to me—in fact, they look kinda drab. I figured the pretty ones, the ones from them places with weird names like Umm al Qaiwan, Bhutan, Malawi—hell, who's ever heard of those places anyway?—were the good ones."

I chuckled. Slocum was sitting on a goldmine, delighted with the fool's gold, not the real thing.

"The dogs and cats aren't really worth too much."

"Is that right? You could have fooled me. You mean that other stuff is pretty good?"

"Yes. I'd like to buy it."

"Great! What's your offer?"

I ran through the figures on my yellow legal pad to make sure I'd added correctly.

"Looks like about nineteen thousand dollars."

Slocum let out a long, slow whistle. "Did you hear that, honey?" he said, turning his head toward the kitchen where Cheri was going about her business. "Man says Gramps' collection is worth nineteen thousand dollars!"

Cheri walked into the living room, wiping her hands on a faded apron. "I had no idea," she said.

I wondered if they were going to accept my offer.

"That's one helluva lot of money. We could even get a boat with that," Slocum said.

I wondered where they would sail a boat out in the middle of nowhere.

"We could fix up the house," Cheri said.

"Hell, we could move!" Slocum said. "You're talking about nineteen with three zeros behind it, right?"

"Yes, nineteen thousand," I said.

"What do you think, honey? Should we take it?"

"Well . . . I guess so."

"Looks like you bought yourself some stamps, mister. Say, how much is that album with all them butterflies worth?"

"About twenty dollars."

"Would you mind if I keep it?"

"No, go right ahead." I wrote up a bill of sale and made out a check while Les Slocum searched the first box for the butterfly album. When he had found it, he sat back on the sofa and began leafing through it.   He looked like a grizzly bear holding a children's book.

It was three o'clock when we finished. Slocum helped me pack the boxes into my station wagon, then shook my hand with his bear trap of a fist.

On the way back, I couldn't help think how odd it was that a collection of the quality of Cheri Slocum's grandfather's would turn up in a tiny house in an out-of-the-way place like Walden, Colorado. But then, if you passed Les Slocum on the street, he would be the last one you'd ever suspect of finding pleasure in an album of butterfly stamps.

Such are the mysteries that make the stamp business so fascinating.

Chapter 20

Mrs. Carleen Griggs—not her real name—lived in Montana and wanted me to come to her home to make an offer on her late husband's collection. From her description, the collection sounded medium sized, large enough to merit interest, but not large enough to make a special trip for. After my experience in Billings, Montana, I had no desire to go on another wild goose chase, so I suggested she send the collection to me or bring it to Denver. She didn't want to do either.

"If you'll leave your number, I'll give you a call when I'm going to be in your neighborhood," I suggested. Sometimes, a couple of collections in the same vicinity will justify a trip. She agreed.

A few weeks later, Matt Daly, a fellow local stamp dealer, mentioned that he was driving to a show in Idaho the next weekend.

"How would you like to look at a collection in Bozeman, Montana?" I asked.

"Sure."

"I'll pay you a ten percent commission if you buy it, or you pay me ten percent and keep it, or I'll split it with you—whatever's fair."

"Great."

"The lady's name is Griggs. I'll call and let her know you'll be getting in touch." I gave Daly her telephone number, and he made an appointment with her.

I didn't think anything more about it until Daly called me from the show in Idaho late Saturday afternoon.

"Business is lousy," he said. "I haven't even taken in a hundred bucks. And no one's paying cash, nothing but nickel-and-dime checks. Right now, I'm hoping to make enough to take care of the motel bill. I hope there'll be enough left over to buy gas for the trip to Bozeman."

"You didn't take any cash with you?"

"Well, I'm a little short at the moment. I figured the show would generate some."

Daly was he was having financial problems, but I was unaware of it.

He had once bounced a check on me for $30,000, claiming the overdraft had been caused by his bank putting an unexpected hold on a large out-of-town check. Perhaps I should have been suspicious, but he had made it good right away with a cashier's check. He'd been embarrassed by the incident and very apologetic, so I didn't give it a second thought.

Matt Daly had an unquenchable passion for stamps, and for deals. I once invited him along with me to value a portion of a large new issue stock that contained a strong sub-section of stamps in his specialty. If the deal closed, he was to have the stamps in the section he had evaluated.

The stock was gorgeous—dozens of file drawers loaded with glassines full of new issues. It had been put together by a man who intended to become a stamp dealer after he retired. Unfortunately, he had died of a heart attack before reaching retirement age. For nearly two decades, the man had bought five to ten sets of every new issue from dozens of Western European, British Commonwealth, and Asian countries. Daly's eyes lit up when he saw the thousands of glassines of mint never hinged sets and singles. He reminded me of a child in toyland at Christmas.

The entire accumulation totaled $20,000 net, but Daly's end was only $1,500. The appraisal proceeded smoothly, and I bought the stock. It took Daly and me several trips to load everything into my car. As we worked, Daly started hinting that he wanted to buy the whole lot. I didn't pay much attention because I thought he understood I intended to keep everything except the section he had appraised.

But he persisted, and back at my office, after we'd finished moving the stock in, said earnestly, "Look, I'm really serious about buying the whole lot. I'm not fooling."

"But I want to break it down for stock," I said. "It's too good an accumulation to turn over for a quick five or ten percent."

"Name your price."

"I don't want to sell."

"C'mon, everything's for sale. Name your price."

"You know what I paid for it, and you know I don't want to sell. But you keep insisting that I name a figure, so I will. Just don't be upset when you hear it. I'm telling you this because it's an outrageous price. I want you to understand that it's outrageous because I *really* don't want to sell."

"Okay, okay," he said, impatiently. "What's your figure?"

I picked a figure out of thin air, confident it was so exorbitant that he would choke and sputter, but pass and finally put the matter to rest.

"Thirty thousand dollars," I said, arranging the boxes.

"Done!" he cried without hesitation.

I was dumbstruck. He had called my bluff, except it wasn't a bluff. I didn't want to sell.

"I'll write you a check."

"But I don't want to sell."

"Nevertheless, we've got a deal. You named your price. I took it."

I should have been happy, having made $10,000 for a morning's work, but I wasn't.

"Oh, come on, Matt—"

"A deal's a deal," he said, handing me the check. "Can I borrow your dolly to move this stuff out to my car?"

I helped him load the boxes, protesting every step of the way. *How can he afford to pay so much?* I kept asking myself. I didn't have a clue.

Daly's $30,000 check had bounced, but as I said, he made it good right away, so I didn't think much of it.

A few weeks later, I asked him how the lot had turned out, curious to know what treasures it might have contained that I had missed.

"Nowhere as good as I thought it would be," Daly said. "I'll get my money out of it, but that's about all."

His remark made me feel better. From the sound of it, I would have made no more by piecemealing it over the long haul, and I'd saved having to invest labor in it. Later, Maggie, Daly's wife, complained that Matt probably would lose a couple thousand on the deal. I think she was implying that I had taken advantage of him.

"What are you going to do?" I asked, suddenly worried as I spoke to Daly the Saturday afternoon he called from Idaho. "How were you going to pay for the collection?"

"Well, I figured if I bought it, I'd give her a check, then drive straight back to Denver and cover it with the check you'd give me. Or you could give Maggie a check, and she'd deposit it."

If I had known how shaky Daly was, I would never have invited him in on the deal. But now things were in motion, so I decided to make the best of it.

"Okay, that would work," I said. "Give me a call if you buy it, and I'll make sure the money's here."

"Thanks, I knew I could count on you. But what if I don't take in enough cash to pay for the motel and gas?"

"Can't you cash some of the checks you've taken in? Or borrow a hundred bucks from one of the guys?"

"I don't think anybody's taken in a hundred—it's been that kind of show, but I'll see what I can do."

"If worse comes to worse, I'll wire you the cash. There's got to be a Western Union office up there."

"Thanks. I'll be in touch."

I was sure he'd call back for cash. Saturday is typically the busiest day of a show; Sundays are notoriously slow. He'd taken in less than a hundred dollars Saturday, so I doubted Sunday would solve his problem.

Daly had planned to drive to Bozeman Monday, look at the collection that afternoon, then head back to Denver the next morning. I didn't hear from him Sunday, so I assumed he had raised enough cash to get to Bozeman. I didn't hear from him Monday, either. Tuesday, I called Maggie to see if she had heard from him. Yes, he had called. He'd had car trouble, but everything was okay. It would take a day or two to fix. He planned to be back by Thursday at the latest.

Friday morning, Daly popped into my office.

"Some trip," he said. "The show was a bust, the car broke down, and Carleen—Mrs. Griggs—decided to keep the collection. It was no big deal anyway, maybe fifteen hundred bucks, but she wanted to keep it a while. Said she'd think it over."

"At least you got an appraisal fee out of it."

"Not exactly . . ." Daly smiled. I wondered what he meant.

"It's a long story. My car broke down about ten miles outside town. I was lucky—it could have happened a hundred miles out. I hitched a ride into town, had the car towed into the local garage. Then I called Carleen. She came right over and picked me up. Real nice lady, late thirties, I'd guess, and friendly, too. I figured I might as well get started on the collection while the car was being fixed.

"The garage man called me at Carleen's and gave me the bad news. The fuel pump had gone out, and he didn't have the right one in stock. He'd have to order one. The earliest he could have the car ready was the next afternoon. I told him to go ahead and fix it—I didn't have any choice. I was going to ask Carleen if she'd cash a check for me, but didn't want to mention it until I'd had chance to look at the collection and get to know her a little better.

"I spent the afternoon going over the collection. When I'd finished, Carleen offered me a drink, then we went out for dinner. We talked about the stamp business, and I told her how crummy the weekend show had been compared to the big-time—New York, Los Angeles, etc. She was fascinated by the stories and the places I'd been. Said she'd never been far from Montana, said life could get pretty dull around there.

"We really hit it off, so I didn't feel too embarrassed when I asked if she could cash a check for me. 'No problem,' she said. I asked her to recommend a good motel. ' Don't be silly,' she said, 'stay at my place.' So, I did."

I shook my head.

Daly grinned. "Who am I to refuse someone's hospitality?"

"And . . . ?"

"We got back to her place, had a few drinks . . . ah . . . and one thing led to another." He grinned. Daly was young, good-looking, and charming. The sort people like immediately. And apparently, Carleen Griggs had taken an instant liking to him. Maggie would be furious if she knew.

"Some friend," I said, shaking my head. "Give you a lead, and not only do you *not* buy the collection, but have a big party instead."

Daly continued grinning, as if immensely pleased with himself.

"What about the appraisal fee?" I asked.

"How could I ask her for an appraisal fee after all her . . . hospitality?"

I saw his point.

"Car didn't get fixed until Wednesday," Daly continued. "I had to stay an extra night, but I didn't mind. Carleen even lent me enough money to cover the car repair and buy gas to get home."

Again, all I could do was shake my head.

"Hey, she might sell the collection someday," he added defensively.

"And I suppose you'll drive back up to get it?"

"Why not? We've got good rapport."

"You're incorrigible!"

Daly grinned. "Hey, I'm just a humble stamp dealer trying to get by."

Right, I thought, *you go to the hinterlands and wind up having a party. I go and end up in the MGM Grand Motel.*

Chapter 21

I met Donovan Kurtz at ORCOEXPO in Los Angeles. He walked up, looked at my table display for a few minutes, then asked, pointing at a large die proof, "Do you have any others?" Kurtz, tall and lean, was in his late fifties. His thinning hair was combed straight back and flat against his skull. He smiled, but his tone was businesslike.

"Yes," I said, reaching behind me for the rest of my stock. Kurtz carefully looked at one after another, separating them into two piles, the smaller of which I assumed he would buy. I was surprised when he handed me the larger stack, saying, "I'll take these."

I added his selections quickly. They totaled $20,875.

"Any discount for volume?" he asked.

"How about twenty thousand for the lot?"

"Okay," he said, reaching into his jacket for a checkbook. "Will a check be all right?"

"Can you give me a reference—someone here at the show?"

"Why don't you check with Stan or Mort? I'm sure they'll vouch for me."

"Okay," I said, stepping out from behind my booth, "Be back in a minute."

Stan's booth was at the end of the aisle. "A fellow name Kurtz wants to give me a check for twenty grand. He said you could vouch for him."

"His check's good as gold," Stan replied.

"You're sure?"

"Absolutely," he said. Then added, "You know who Kurtz is, don't you?"

I shook my head. I had no idea.

"You've heard of Kurtz Capital Corporation?"

I shrugged. I had never heard of it.

"Finances oil deals, takes over companies, that kind of stuff."

"Sorry, doesn't ring a bell."

"Well, take my word for it, his check's good."

I trusted Stan, so I returned to my booth, mind at ease.

"Do you have any more proofs?" Kurtz asked.

"Some, but not many."

"Why don't you call me when you get back to your office. I'd be interested to know what you have." He handed me his check.

"I'll do that," I said, looking first at the check, then at Kurtz. "Do you have a card?"

He handed me a simple engraved card. I gave him one of mine.

Donovan Kurtz had just made my show. Even if I didn't make another sale, I would come away with an excellent profit.

The following week, Kurtz bought another $1,500 worth of proofs by phone. He said he was starting a proof collection and was interested in buying any he didn't have. I promised to call him if any others came in. Then, I forgot all about him.

A few weeks later, he called.

"Got any plans this afternoon?" he asked

"No," I replied, thinking he might be in town and wanted to drop by.

"Good. Why don't you fly out to Las Vegas, and we'll have dinner tonight?"

"Las Vegas?" I didn't know what to say, so I said, "I thought you lived in Los Angeles."

"I do, but I'm in Las Vegas looking at some property, and, since it's less than a two-hour flight from Denver, I though it might be a convenient spot for us to get together. I've got something important I'd like to talk to you about."

His invitation caught me off guard, but before I could say anything further, he continued.

"The trip, the hotel, and dinner are on me. There's a Continental flight leaving at about two. We'll have dinner tonight, you can catch a return flight first thing tomorrow, and be back in your office by noon."

"Can't we discuss it on the phone?"

"No, Mr. Datz. As I said, it's important, and I prefer to discuss important matters face-to-face."

I couldn't imagine what business we might have that was so important it required a face-to-face meeting—in Las Vegas.

"There'll be a ticket waiting for you at the Continental counter at the airport. As I said, the trip's on me."

Las Vegas. An unexpected call from a wealthy, enigmatic businessman. A $20,000 sale a few weeks earlier. Something important that could only be discussed face-to-face. Suddenly, I knew I had to go.

"Okay, I'll fly down."

"Good, Mr. Datz, good. I'm staying at the Tropicana. It's close to the airport. Check with the front desk when you arrive. There'll be a room waiting for you. Call me when you get in. I'm looking forward to seeing you again."

"I'll call you when I get there," I said.

I drove home right away and tried to explain the puzzling invitation to my wife, Sue, as she hurriedly packed an overnight bag for me.

"It sounds kind of peculiar," she said. "What's so important that you have to drop everything and rush down to Las Vegas? Who is this guy Kurtz, anyway?"

I couldn't give her a meaningful answer. I didn't know myself.

A ticket was waiting at the Continental counter at Stapleton Airport, just as Kurtz had said. Once aboard the plane, I settled back in my seat and spent the whole flight wondering what Donovan Kurtz could possibly want. Perhaps Kurtz, the millionaire, was in the market for an agent, someone discreet, someone to sniff out exceptional stamps. Wealthy collectors, lacking time and preferring anonymity, sometimes hire knowledgeable professionals to locate stamps for them. I imagined myself traveling the nation—even the world—scouring shows, auctions, and dealers for elusive rarities.

"Privacy," I imagined Kurtz saying. "A man in my position values privacy above all else."

"I understand," I reply.

"Find the stamps, pay whatever you have to, but buy them," Kurtz says. "Money is no object."

"Yes, sir!" I say. I imagine myself bidding $100,000 for a stamp, maybe even $1,000,000 for the ultimate rarity.

"Who is your anonymous client?" everyone wants to know.

"Sorry, I'd love to tell you, but I can't," I say, savoring the intrigue. I could see it clearly in my mind as I reclined in my seat on the way to Las Vegas. I tried to nap, but couldn't escape the relentless grip of the daydream, my rendezvous with destiny.

I arrived in Las Vegas, checked into the Tropicana, and called Kurtz's room. He was out. I left a message that I would be back at 4:30. Then, I went to the casino. I had noticed its bright lights, heard the steady murmur of action when I checked in. I wanted a closer look. As I strolled through the casino, I spotted Donovan Kurtz at a craps table.

"Ah, glad to see you made it, Mr. Datz," he said, greeting me. "I trust you had a pleasant trip?"

"Very smooth."

"And your room is satisfactory?"

"Very nice, thank you." *Very nice* was an understatement. The suite was first-class.

"I'd like you to meet Henderson Quayle," he said, introducing me to a small, thin, well-dressed man standing attentively to his left. I stepped behind Kurtz and shook Quayle's hand. Quayle was Kurtz's executive aide-de-camp.

"I'll be finished here shortly," Kurtz said, "But first, I've got to follow a hunch."

I knew little about craps, but the action intrigued me.

"The young woman at the far end of the table was very lucky last time she had the dice. She was very good to me," Kurtz said softly, patting the chips in the counter rack in front of him. The rack was loaded with chips: a few green $25 chips, twenty or thirty black $100 chips, and dozens of white $500 chips.

"There's a school of thought that holds that you look for winners, then bet with them. I have a hunch that young woman is a winner," Kurtz said, "and I like to play my hunches."

"New shooter coming out," the stickman announced in his carnival pitchman's voice. "Get your bets down, big red, C&E." I had no idea what he was talking about, but the players responded enthusiastically, plunking chips down all over the board.

At the far end of the table, an animated young woman with short, raven-black hair and dazzling blue eyes dropped a red $5 chip on the pass line. The stickman pushed five dice toward her. She chose two and, shaking them vigorously, implored, "Come on, baby! Come on, seven! Don't disappoint me! You can do it, c'mon!"

The dice sailed across the table toward us and bounced off the siderail, rolling in slow motion—it seemed—until a two and five showed.

"*All-right!*" the young woman shouted, snapping her fingers, bouncing up and down. "All-right!"

"Win-nah! Pay the line," the stickman chanted, as he gathered the dice with his stick and pulled them over to the boxman, who supervised the game from his seat behind the currency drop.

One of the dealers—whose job it is to keep track of the action, assist players, and settle bets—pushed out two white chips to match the two Kurtz had on the pass line. He had just won $1,000. Kurtz ignored the winnings, and the dealer, as if by silent signal, placed the two white chips on top of the original bet. Kurtz now had $2,000 riding on the next roll.

The young woman, too, let her chips ride—all $10 worth.

The stickman pushed the dice across the green felt toward her. They matched the ruby color of her fingernails. She grasped them in her small white hand and shook them.

"Come on, baby! Magic seven! You can do it!" she said, and let fly. Again, the dice flew across the table toward us, bounced and rolled. Up came a three and a four.

"*Yy-eee-sss!*" she cried, bouncing on the balls of her feet, clapping her hands. The ecstacy of winning danced in her bright blue eyes, and her face beamed, as brilliantly as the neon that blazed everywhere in Las Vegas.

"Win-nah! Pay the line," the stickman chanted.

Suddenly, the table seemed crowded, and everyone wanted to get a bet down.

"There's something about beautiful women," Kurtz said, quietly, "that makes people want to bet on them." He smiled. "Many men have lost a lot of money that way . . . but I have a hunch she's a winner."

The dealer pushed out four more $500 chips to match the four Kurtz had wagered. Again, Kurtz ignored his winnings. It was clear he wanted to let them ride. This time, however, the dealer made no move to place them on top of the other chips. The table limit was $3,000, $1,000 less than Kurtz's accumulated winnings. The dealer looked toward the boxman, who turned and looked toward the manager, who—suddenly attracted by the flurry of action—was standing behind him. The manager nodded as if nothing exceptional was taking place.

"Four thousand, take it," the boxman said barely audibly, and the dealer dutifully stacked Kurtz's chips on the pass line.

The young woman let her chips ride, also—all $20 worth.

"The lady's hot," the stickman chanted, "Get your bets down." Eager players crowded the betting rail, wanting to get in on the action. Most bets were small, $5, $10, $25, but a couple of black hundred-dollar chips appeared on the table. I suddenly realized that all the other chips on the table didn't amount to a fraction of Kurtz's wager. Kurtz remained cool and nonchalant.

The stickman pushed the dice toward the spirited young woman. "All bets down. Hands up," he said, warning everyone to get their hands out of the path of the dice. The young woman exhorted the dice once again and let fly. They rolled and bounced. One hit Kurtz's stack of chips, knocking a couple off the top, and came to rest showing a two. The other ricocheted off the siderail, landing behind the dealer's stacks of chips. Heads craned to see the result, also a two.

"Four the hard way. Four, the point," the stickman chanted.

I knew the young woman would have to roll a four—the point—before rolling a seven, or she would lose. There are six ways to roll a seven, but only three ways to roll a four. The odds favored a seven coming up before a four. *Kurtz should have taken his $4,000 while he had the chance,* I thought. But he remained indifferent. Instead, he counted out a pile of white chips and dropped them on the table.

The attentive dealer reached for them asking, "Cover the board, Mr. K?"

Kurtz nodded. By my rough count, Kurtz had more than $7,000 riding on the next roll of the dice. *The dealer called him Mr. K,* I thought. *He must be well known here. Who is this man, Donovan Kurtz?*

The young woman rolled. A six popped up. The dealer's hands gathered chips, stacked them, moved them around, all with amazing speed and dexterity. He shoved a stack toward Kurtz, asking, "Press, Mr. K?"

Kurtz shook his head, and Quayle picked up the chips and racked them. The blue-eyed young woman rolled again and again, but neither a four nor a seven came up. On every roll, Kurtz's board bets paid off, and Quayle racked his chips.

The assembled bettors, like fans rooting for the home team, cheered the young woman on. "Think four, honey! You can't miss!"

She grabbed the dice, but before rolling, flashed a blinding smile at her cheering boosters, now crowded elbow-to-elbow around the table—and they loved it. "C'mon, pretty blue eyes, show 'em how it's done!" the man next to her whooped. Even though I had no money on the table, I, too, found myself swept up in the emotion, silently cheering, *C'mon, blue-eyes, you can do it!* Only Kurtz, the boxman, and the manager remained impassive.

With each roll, the stickman chanted his patter, and the dealer's fingers scurried to pay off winners and collect losses. Suspense mounted. The crowd knew that odds favored a seven, favored the young woman losing. But the crowd pulled for her, the way fans pull for a batter in the bottom of the ninth with bases loaded, two outs, and the score tied.

A short, stocky man with big beefy fists and a sweat-stained baseball cap tossed two $25 chips to the stickman. "Fifty on seven," he said. Seven paid five-to-one odds, and, he reasoned, it was long overdue to come up. Several players frowned. They didn't appreciate anyone betting against their favorite—it was bad luck. Again and again, the stocky man dropped $50 on the table, sure that the blue-eyed woman's luck had run out. But she ate him alive, one $50 bite after another, until at last he'd had enough and quit, $250 dollars lighter.

"Never seen nothing like it!" he said, sheepishly, aware that the crowd was glad he had lost, that he had been punished for betting against the home town batter.

Just when it seemed it could go on no longer, the stickman announced, "Four, the easy way! Win-nah on a short roll! Pay the line. Pay the field."

The table erupted in shouts that could be heard all over the casino. The manager shook his head and snorted in disbelief. The boxman looked up at him and shrugged.

The young blue-eyed woman had won $20. Kurtz had won at least a thousand times that much.   She was ecstatic.   Kurtz remained cool and impassive.

"Down my bets," he said quietly to the dealer, indicating that his bets were off.   "I'm taking a break."

"Yes, sir, Mr. K," the dealer replied.

He tossed a white $500 chip in the direction of the boxman and said, "Thanks, fellas."

"Yes, sir, *thank you,* Mr. K," the boxman replied with a nod of respect.

"Come, Mr. Datz," Kurtz said, "Join me for a drink."   As we strolled toward the lounge, he said, "The secret is in knowing when to walk away."

"Aren't you going to collect your chips?" I asked.

"Henderson will take care of that," he said, smiling.

We took seats in the lounge. Kurtz ordered a scotch, I had a gin and tonic.

"I'm curious about why you asked me to fly to Las Vegas."

"There's something I want to talk to you about." Then, as if he had just remembered something, he pulled out a leather-covered Daytimer and made a note in it.

"Yes, sir, Mr. Datz, we have business," he repeated, tucking the Daytimer into his jacket pocket, "but all in good time."

The cocktail waitress arrived and served our drinks.

"How are things at Scott Publishing?" he said, raising his glass in a perfunctory toast.

"Just fine," I said, acknowledging his toast with my glass.

"According to your card, you're vice president of Scott. I was surprised by the Denver address. I thought Scott Publishing was headquartered in New York." He took a small sip of scotch, the glass barely touching his lips.

"It is. I'm vice president of Scott Philatelic," I said. "Scott has three divisions—Scott Publishing, Scott Auction Gallery, and Scott Philatelic. I'm in charge of Scott Philatelic."

The gin and tonic tasted sweet. I fished the wedge of lime from the drink and squeezed it, adding more tartness.

"Each division is set up as a separate corporation. Scott Publishing publishes the catalogues, and manufactures albums and supplies. Scott Auction is involved strictly in auctioning stamps. Scott Philatelic is relatively new and based in Denver. We buy and sell stamps, travel to shows, and represent the interests of Scott Collectibles—the parent of the three divisions—in the west."

"I see," Kurtz said thoughtfully, taking another sip of scotch.

Scott Philatelic had been set up in the late 1970s at a time when Scott Collectibles decided to diversify and to get back into the business of buying and selling stamps. In 1984 Amos Press bought Scott and decided to forgo both auctioning and selling stamps, preferring to concentrate on the publishing end of the business. But, at the time I shared a drink with Donovan Kurtz, that was still in the distant future.

The man seated across from me sipping scotch was an enigma. Except for his buying more than $20,000 worth of stamps from me as casually as one might pick up a magazine off a newsstand, or that I had just seen him win more than $20,000 a few minutes earlier, I knew nothing about him. I wondered what he wanted.

"What do you collect?" I asked.

"Oh, a little bit of this, a little bit of that," he said, smiling. Then, more seriously, "I've had a lifelong ambition of owning a complete collection of U.S. stamps."

"That's quite a goal," I said, stirring my gin and tonic with a swizzle stick. As a youngster, I had added up the cost of acquiring every U.S. stamp—not counting all the reissues—and had been surprised to learn the sum ran into six figures. The revelation had hit me like a bucket of cold water. Collecting was never the same after I realized I couldn't complete my collection mowing lawns.

"Well, I'm pretty far along," he said modestly, at least I took it as modesty because there was no trace of pretentiousness in his voice.

"Do you exhibit?" I asked.

"No, I'm afraid not. Don't think I'd do very well, besides, I prefer to keep a low profile. I don't enjoy the limelight."

"So, how can I help you?" I asked, still wondering why he had invited me to Las Vegas.

"We'll get to that, Mr. Datz. Yes sir, we'll get to that," he said, sipping his scotch, leveling his eyes at me. They seemed friendly enough, but distant.

"I thought it would be nice to get acquainted first. I like to know a little about the men with whom I deal," he said. "What do you collect, Mr. Datz?"

"A little bit of this, a little bit of that," I said, stirring my drink.

"Touché, Mr. Datz," he said with a chuckle, raising his glass. *"Touché.* I like a man with a sense of humor. Indeed, I do. I can see we're going to get along well."

"I'm still curious about why you invited me to Las Vegas."

"We'll get to that, Mr. Datz, all in good time. Meanwhile, let's get acquainted."

I decided to stop pressing the issue. Kurtz was, no doubt, sizing me up before committing himself to an arrangement. Donovan Kurtz was a shrewd, wealthy man, and shrewd men don't get wealthy by making rash decisions.

We chatted for fifteen or twenty minutes, then, looking at his watch, Kurtz said, "Please excuse me, Mr. Datz. I have to make a few phone calls. We'll talk more at dinner."

"Fine," I said, draining the last of my drink.

"How about six-thirty at the Bacchanal? Marvelous food, fit for a king. It's in Caesars Palace, just down the strip."

"Sounds fine."

"I'd be glad to give you a lift, unless you'd rather walk and see some of the town before dinner."

"I think I'll do that," I said. "I'll meet you at six-thirty at the restaurant."

"Okay, see you then." Kurtz walked away, reaching inside his jacket for his Daytimer.

I went to my room, freshened up, then wandered around the Tropicana for a while, watching the blackjack players, the craps tables, and the roulette wheels. In an elevated corner nook, men clad in formal wear and women in elegant evening wear relaxed at the baccarat table. I imagined James Bond matching wits with Goldfinger.

The casino was decorated in a tropical motif: splashes of sunlit emerald next to patches of dark brooding jungle green, bright orchid pinks next to dusky purples, all in floral patterns that repeated themselves like entities from an M. C. Escher print. Above casino players rose a high, vaulted ceiling decorated in stained glass, yellows and browns and pale golds. It looked like a cathedral, except that instead of angels, topless beauties smiled down on the assembled gamblers, all to the steady, metallic rat-a-tat-tat of coins dropping into metal trays beneath the slot machines.

I walked past the craps table where earlier Kurtz had won a small fortune. I thought about dinner and what Kurtz might have in mind. The world of philately suddenly seemed glamorous, mysterious, and exciting.

I set out for Caesars Palace. It was only a few blocks away, but, I quickly learned, blocks in Las Vegas are larger than long blocks in Manhattan, or so it seemed. Had I known how long a walk it was and how sore my feet would get, I would have gotten a ride.

I toured casinos along the way and learned that, except for motif, they're essentially the same: a few roulette wheels, a few craps tables, plenty of blackjack tables, and hundreds, perhaps thousands, of slot machines. The casinos were crowded with men and women, young and old, wealthy and poor, beautiful and homely, all side by side, backgrounds, education, and accomplishments irrelevant in the egalitarian pursuit of winning. Despite the glitter and excitement, all I could think about was Donovan Kurtz. What did he want?

I got to Caesars Palace with twenty minutes to spare. My feet were killing me, so I asked to be seated early. When I mentioned Kurtz's name, the maitre d' said, "Ah, yes. Right this way, sir," and ushered me to a plush red-leather booth. It seemed that everyone in town knew Donovan Kurtz—except me.

I didn't have to wait long. Kurtz showed up a few minutes before six-thirty.

"Good to see you," he said, shaking my hand, then he stepped to the other side of the table and seated himself. "Punctuality is a virtue I admire, Mr. Datz." He smiled.

His comment made me feel that I had just passed a test.

"Did you visit the casinos up and down the street?"

"They're quite impressive."

A smiling woman clad in a skimpy harem outfit arrived and poured wine into our chalices—from shoulder height.

"Have any luck?" Kurtz asked after the pause.

"I'm afraid I'm not much of a gambler."

"Probably a wise policy, Mr. Datz," he said, smiling. "However, risk holds a certain fascination for me. There is risk in business, risk in love—in fact, life is all about risk, Mr. Datz. Life is a gamble, a balance of risk against profit. The gaming tables simply compress the factor of time. You learn immediately if your intuition was correct."

From anyone else, Kurtz's philosophical comments might have sounded boastful or preachy, but considering his wealth and success, they struck me as important—points worth noting. I felt like an novice listening to a great sage.

"That philosophy seems to have worked well for you," I said. Kurtz smiled. "What is it that your firm does?"

"I venture capital, help get companies started, help them grow, offer advice on how markets operate, even buy ailing firms and try to restore them to health. I'm just a small cog in the great engine of commerce."

The waiter arrived and took our dinner order.

"I think I mentioned that I've had a lifelong ambition of putting together a complete collection of U.S. stamps."

"Yes, you did."

"Well, Mr. Datz, I've been at it for many years. I've been rather picky about what I buy. I've always demanded quality because I felt that anything worth doing, is worth doing right—eh?"

I nodded.

"I have managed to acquire every single U.S. stamp . . . except one." Kurtz paused, took another sip of wine, let his words sink in. And they did—I had never known anyone who had a complete collection of U.S. stamps.

"You must be lacking the one-cent Z grill," I said.

"Right you are, Mr. Datz, right you are." He seemed pleased that I had guessed correctly. "And who knows when—or if—I'll ever own it. But that's beside the point—my real passion is banknotes. Got interested in them along the way, and lucky, too, because if not for them, I'd have nothing to keep me busy once my general collection was as far along as it is.

"I've studied banknotes extensively," he said. "I've got every variety listed in Scott, again, except one, and that's my problem. It's something I hope you can help me with."

From the sound of it, Kurtz had an extremely advanced collection, doubtlessly put together with the assistance of the oldest and best firms in the business. If they hadn't been able to locate his elusive banknote, I doubted I could either. Kurtz, I judged, was the kind of man who expected results, and I didn't want to undertake something I couldn't deliver on.

"I'm sure you've had major dealers on both coasts keeping an eye open for the stamp," I said. "I don't think there's much more I can do, but I'll be happy to try. I must tell you right up front, though, not to get your hopes up."

"Nothing would please me more, Mr. Datz, than if you could find that stamp. But, frankly, I don't think you're going have any better luck than the others."

Then, why the trip, I thought. *Why drag me to Las Vegas to tell me about a stamp you don't think I'll be able to find?*

Kurtz paused and took another sip of wine.

"I doubt you'd have any better luck than the others, Mr. Datz, because the stamp doesn't exist."

"I'm afraid you've lost me. If the stamp doesn't exist, why bother with it?"

He chuckled. He paused while our salads were served.

"I've been chasing this stamp for years—with no luck. And I've concluded that it doesn't exist. That's where you can help me."

He paused again, as if weighing carefully what he was about to say.

"You can delete the stamp from your catalogue," he said, at last, looking directly at me. "Then, my collection will be complete." He continued gazing at me for a long moment, then returned to his salad, sawing a small tomato in half with his knife.

I was astonished. What a novel way to complete a collection—have the missing stamp delisted! How exquisitely bizarre.

"I've talked with all the old timers—collectors and dealers. No one recalls ever seeing the stamp. Lester Brookman makes no mention of it in his book, nor does any other reference. I've looked through hundreds—maybe thousands—of old auction catalogues going back decades, and never once has this variety appeared at auction. I don't think it exists—period." He took a bite of salad.

"Even if you're right, there's not much I can do for you," I said. "I'm not in the catalogue department. I have no power to include or exclude anything from the catalogue."

"Still, you *are* with the company. Couldn't you talk to someone in the catalogue department about it? If the stamp doesn't exist, certainly it doesn't justify a listing."

"Perhaps not, but you should contact the catalogue department directly. I'd be happy to give you the name of the man to talk to."

"I've written letters, but never gotten a response. I'm sure they think I'm some sort of crank. Perhaps if you mentioned it, they might consider it more seriously."

"I could, but I really doubt it would do much good. You'd need solid proof to get a listing changed. Even then, it wouldn't be easy."

"I suspect the listing got in a long time ago, back in the early days before catalogue editors were as stringent as they are today. I've heard that in those days stamps occasionally were listed on someone's say-so, even if the man reporting an item's existence hadn't actually seen it himself. I think my missing banknote is one of those."

"Well, as far as I know, the policy is that, once something's in the catalogue, it stays in unless there's overwhelming evidence to the contrary. It's like precedent in law. Once a precedent is on the books, it's very difficult to change."

"But not impossible?" Kurtz looked at me, waiting for me to agree. I shrugged.

"Doesn't it stand to reason that, if the listing is in error, it should be corrected?"

"I suppose so, but there's the matter of proof."

"If none of the experts have ever seen it, if it's never appeared at auction, isn't that pretty good evidence that it doesn't exist?"

"Perhaps, but it's circumstantial, at best. What if a copy shows up tomorrow?"

"Nothing would please me more. I'd buy it! But I don't really think one will."

The conversation paused for a moment.

"If you're convinced the stamp doesn't exist, why not just ignore it?" I asked.

"I could, but the catalogue is the basis for defining complete-ness. Technically, I won't have a complete collection as long as the stamp is listed. I'd just like to see the record set straight . . . and be able to complete my collection," he said with a sigh.

Perhaps Kurtz's phantom banknote existed, perhaps not. I didn't know. He sounded sincere and impressed me as a man who had carefully studied his specialty and honestly believed the catalogue to be in error. Still, I knew in my heart that the catalogue department wouldn't change a listing without incontrovertible evidence.

"I'd hoped you might be a little more encouraging, Mr. Datz," Kurtz said as our main course arrived. "I'm not a man who gives up easily—no sir, I am not." He put a knife to his steak.

Sitting across from Donovan Kurtz, it occurred to me that he was the kind of man who could buy Scott Publishing Company—if he wanted to—just to set the record straight as he saw it.

We finished our dinners, one of the most sumptuous I'd ever had, and enjoyed pastries, cheese, and fruit. I promised to talk to the catalogue department about his phantom stamp, but I made it clear that he shouldn't get his hopes up. He seemed to understand and thanked me.

"Would you like a ride back to the Trop?" Kurtz asked, when we had finished.

"That would be great," I said, my feet aching with every step I took.

Next morning, I rose at six and prepared to depart. The moment I walked out the front door of the Tropicana, I felt soft desert air on my face. Its subtle fragrance made me realize how sterile air-conditioned casino air is. It's the difference between freshly squeezed orange juice and Kool-Aid.

I looked up at the gleaming hotel towers. Somewhere—probably near the top floor—Donovan Kurtz was ensconced in a VIP suite.

"Airport?" the doorman asked.

I nodded.

"Just a couple minutes."

I put my overnight bag down and waited. The sun was still below the horizon. Overhead, wisps of peach-gold streaked the pale early-morning sky. To the west, the distant hills slumbered, still snug in their bedding of deep violets and dark purples.

As I waited for the shuttle, I glanced again and again at the tower. It fascinated me, as did Kurtz. I thought about his passion for stamps, his success and wealth, and how his prize eluded him. I thought about what he had said: "Life is a gamble." The words struck me as profound, but I wasn't sure I believed him. Or perhaps I wasn't sufficiently wise to recognize and appreciate a universal truth. Only much later, when a fellow dealer questioned the wisdom of making trips to follow up shaky leads, did I realize that I, too, was a risk taker, that each trip was a gamble. Suddenly, I understood what Donovan Kurtz had meant.

Soon, I would be in the air on my way back to Denver. I would refer Kurtz's request to the catalogue department. Time would pass and nothing would happen. The listing that stood between Donovan Kurtz and the goal of completing his stamp collection would remain in the catalogue.

But I didn't know those things as I stood in front of the Tropicana waiting for the airport shuttle. The morning was so mild and the desert so serene, that I wished I had my car. It was a perfect day for a leisurely drive across country with nothing but miles and miles of straight, empty road ahead.

Epilogue

"I can't wait until I retire," the middle-aged man had said as he perused my stock. "It's going to be great!"

My first inclination was to say, "You don't know what you're getting into. The show circuit's not a big party. It's a business, and it's not easy. You've got to make a profit or fall by the wayside. You're constantly chasing fresh stock, facing headaches at airports and hotels, risking money on shows that might not break even, worrying about theft, crime, and insurance. Then, there's the unexpected, like the tornado in Dallas. No, sir, life on the road isn't all it's cracked up to be."

But I didn't say those things. Instead, I smiled and said, "Yes, you're going to get a real kick out of it."

It was the right answer because I knew that deep inside the man seated across the table from me lurked the fantasy of every boy who ever dreamed of running away to join the circus, see the world, be a lion tamer, a trapeze artist, or work on the carnival midway. I knew that when he closed his eyes, he smelled hot buttered popcorn, roasted peanuts, and fresh straw. He saw the bright incandescent lights of the midway and heard the hypnotic chant of the pitchman in the Panama hat. He heard the calliope and saw the gypsy jugglers, whose dark eyes danced in the evening light.

"Yes, you're going to love it." I said, because I, too, had been enchanted by the same vision, and I knew that even after the mirage of anticipation vanishes, the power of the road remains irresistible, and the siren song of the carnival keeps calling you on.

OTHER BOOKS BY STEPHEN R. DATZ

If you enjoyed *On The Road,* you'll enjoy *Top Dollar Paid!* and *The Wild Side,* also by Stephen R. Datz.

Told in the same anecdotal style as *On The Road, Top Dollar Paid!* gives insight into the world of stamp dealing and what to expect when you sell.

Besides factual information, the book is loaded with entertaining chapters such as *Fun With Dick & Jane* (what do you do when confronted by a gun-toting seller and his martial arts trained wife?), *You Can't Go Wrong at Face & Other Myths* (what do you do with $234,000 worth of mint sheets?), *Hail to the Chief* (relates Datz's experiences appraising and arranging for auction of President Gerald R. Ford's stamp collection), as well as many others including *Have Check, Will Travel; The Games People Play; Surprise, Surprise, Surprise; Great Expectations; All That Glitters;* and more.

You may not currently be in the market to sell and wonder, "What good is this book to me?" Perhaps the greatest service *Top Dollar Paid!* performs is to make you aware of the future financial consequences of the purchases you're making right now. All stamps are not created equal!

Regardless of whether you're selling today or in ten years, the information in *Top Dollar Paid!* could be worth hundreds or even thousands of dollars to you.

Top Dollar Paid! is really two books in one: a concise guide to what works best in selling, and an entertaining behind-the-scenes journey into the real-life world of stamp dealing. It's been critically acclaimed as the best book ever written on the subject. It's a book you can't afford to be without.

The Wild Side is a journey into the side of stamp dealing you never hear about.

You'll meet a rip-off artist who laughs in his victims' faces–and gets away with it!

You'll meet a flim-flammer who loves people with gold cards. He or others like him could be using your credit cards right now without your knowledge—even if you shred your carbons!

You'll meet a shadowy traveling man who sells stamps too good to be true (regummed, reperfed, etc.) at bargain prices—he may visit your city next. You'll want to beware this stamp man!

You'll meet a murderer who'll chill your blood, and join in the sting when he's caught!

You'll meet a man who boasted about his collection too much—and paid the ultimate price!

You'll meet a genius and a beautiful woman—together with them, you'll attend a bizarre and terrifying seance. It's the strangest experience Datz has ever had in the stamp business!

You'll meet a variety of con men, rascals, scoundrels, eccentrics and characters, and you'll be delightfully entertained by incredible true adventures from a side of philately you never imagined: *The Wild Side!*

One well-known philatelic journalist reported: "There are a lot of lessons to be learned from *The Wild Side.* Now I know how to protect myself against being taken advantage of!"

You won't want to miss *The Wild Side.* Once you start reading, you won't be able to put it down!

Top Dollar Paid! and *The Wild Side* are available at your stamp dealer, bookstore, or you may order directly from the publisher.

Top Dollar Paid! $9.95
The Wild Side $9.95
(Add $2 shipping per order.)

GENERAL PHILATELIC CORPORATION
P. O. Box 402
Loveland, CO 80539